That Said

Books by Jane Shore

A YES-OR-NO ANSWER (2008)

HAPPY FAMILY (1999)

MUSIC MINUS ONE (1996)

THE MINUTE HAND (1987)

EYE LEVEL (1977)

That Said

New and Selected Poems

[signature]

JANE SHORE

To Vijay.

Finally, in person!

xo Jane
Boston
3/20/14

Houghton Mifflin Harcourt
Boston New York 2012

For information about permission to reproduce selections from this book,
write to Permissions, Houghton Mifflin Harcourt Publishing Company,
215 Park Avenue South, New York, New York 10003.
www.hmhbooks.com

Library of Congress Cataloging-in-Publication Data
Shore, Jane, date.
That said : new and selected poems / Jane Shore.
p. cm.
ISBN 978-0-547-68711-7
I. Title.
PS3569.H5795T53 2012
811'.54 — dc23
2011036907

Book design by Greta D. Sibley

Printed in the United States of America
DOC 10 9 8 7 6 5 4 3 2 1

MUSIC MINUS ONE® is a registered trademark of MMO Music Group, Inc.
MMO Music Group has not in any way sponsored, approved, endorsed, or
authorized this book.

Contents

THE MINUTE HAND (1987)

MUSIC MINUS ONE (1996)

They inflict on us a tremendous silence.

—Rainer Maria Rilke, "Some Reflections on Dolls: On the Wax Dolls of Lotte Pritzel"

NEW POEMS

Willow

It didn't weep the way a willow should.
Planted all alone in the middle of the field
by the bachelor who sold our house to us,
shoulder height when our daughter was born,
it grew eight feet a year until it blocked
the view through the first-, then the second-
story windows, its straggly canopy obstructing
our sunrise and moonrise over Max Gray Road.
I gave it the evil eye, hoping lightning
would strike it, the way a bolt had split
the butternut by the barn. And if leaf blight
or crown gall or cankers didn't kill it, then
I'd gladly pay someone to chop it down.
My daughter said no, she loved that tree,
and my husband agreed. One wet Sunday—
the rainiest July since 1885—
husband napping, daughter at a matinee
in town—a wind shear barreled up the hill
so loud I glanced up from my mystery
the moment the willow leaned, bowed,
and fell over flat on its back, roots and all,
splayed on the ground like Gulliver.
The house shook, just once.
Later, when the sun came out, neighbors
came to gawk; they chain-sawed thicker
branches, wrapped chains around the trunk,
their backhoe ripped out pieces of stump
and root as if extracting a rotten tooth.

I'm not sorry that tree is gone. No one
ever sat under it for shade or contemplation.
Yet spring after spring it reliably leafed out.
It was always the last to lose its leaves
in fall. It should have died a decade ago
for all the grief I gave it, my dirty looks
apparently the fuel on which it thrived.
It must have done its weeping in private.
But now I can see the slope of the hill.
Did my wishful thinking cast a spell?
I was the only one on earth who saw it fall.

Priorities

Sleeping alone in my Madison Avenue
Upper East Side seventeen-by-seventeen
fourth-floor walkup one night thirty
years ago, I heard people arguing
through the plaster and brick wall dividing
my brownstone from the one next door.
I'd hardly given my neighbors a second thought
except those I'd occasionally see in the hall
retrieving mail, struggling up narrow stairs
with grocery bags, or leashing their dogs.

I used to amuse myself by matching up faces
with the names above the intercom buttons
in the vestibule downstairs, but I never
stopped for anything more than chitchat,
never thought about the people living
in the adjacent building until the night I hear
a woman crying loud enough to rouse me,
and a deeper voice, a man's, whose words
I can't make out but whose angry bellowing
bullies me awake. Perhaps they're actors

rehearsing a play, or he's her drama coach
and she's practicing her lines from the scene
where the man and the woman fight.
I'm thinking I should dial 911 when—
through the white noise of my hissing radiator—
he shouts, "You've got to order your priorities!"

like a therapist on an emergency house call,
which works. She's whimpering like a dog.
There follows a clearing of the moment's
throat, a sponging of tears, a charged silence,

as if now they're making love and all before
was foreplay. And I'm in bed with them.
How many times have I had to listen—
half attracted, half repelled—to strangers' thumps
and moans in the hotel room next to mine?
Their dramas? The next morning, sharing their
elevator (too bright, too small) to the lobby,
I have nothing to be ashamed of. But I'm feeling
that same tongue-tied strangeness I used to feel
with a one-night stand the morning after.

Fortune Cookies

My old boyfriend's fortune cookie read,
Your love life is of interest only to yourself.
Not news to me. A famous writer
once showed me the fortune in his wallet—
You must curb your lust for revenge—
slapped over his dead mother's face.

After finishing our Chinese meal
at that godforsaken mall,
eight of us crowded around the table,
the white tablecloth sopping up
islands of spilled soy sauce and beer,
the waiter brought tea and oranges
sliced into eighths and a plate of fortune cookies.

We played our after-dinner game—
each of us saying our line out loud,
the chorus adding its coda:
"You will meet hundreds of people..." *"In bed."*
"Every man is a volume if you know how to read him..." *"In bed."*
"You have unusual equipment for success..." *"In bed."*
And those with more delicate sensibilities,
new to the group, blushed
and checked their wristwatches.

We divided up the bill, and split.
A few left their fortunes behind.
The rest slipped those scraps of hope or doom

into pockets and pocketbooks to digest later.
Maybe one or two of us got lucky that night
and had a long and happy life in bed.
On the ride home, I absent-mindedly
rolled my fortune into a tight coil,
the way you roll a joint, and dropped it
into my coat pocket,

and found it yesterday—
oh, how many years later—
caught between the stitches of the seam,
like one of those notes
wedged into a niche of the Wailing Wall
that someday God might read in bed
and change a life.

Chatty Cathy

The first time I got my hands on her,
I took off all her clothes—to see
exactly where her voice came from.
I pulled the white plastic O-ring
knotted to the pull string in her back,
pulled it, gently, as far as it would go,
and Chatty Cathy threw her voice—
not from her closed pretty pink lips
but from the open speaker-grille in her chest.
Chatty Cathy was her own ventriloquist!

She said eighteen phrases at random,
chatting up anyone who'd pull her string.
Tell me a story. Will you play with me?
What can we do now? Do you love me?
Did I love her? I loved her so much
I had to be careful not to wear her out.
Even though she always "talked back,"
behavior my parents would have spanked me for,
there wasn't a naughty bone in her
hard little body! When she'd say,
Carry me. Change my dress. Take me with you.
Brush my hair—she always said *Please*.
When she'd say, *Let's play school.*
Let's have a party. Let's play house—
she'd flash me her charming potbelly.

May I have a cookie? she'd sweetly ask,
in that high fake goody-goody voice.
She wasn't allowed to eat or drink—
it would gunk up the mini record player
inside her chest. *May I have a cookie?*
She'd pester me while I combed her hair
and buttoned her dress for a tea party.
I'm hungry—she'd point her index finger at me until
I held a pretend cookie against her lips
and poured her another empty cup of tea.
May I have a cookie? May I have a cookie?

Finally, one afternoon I gave her one,
squishing it into the holes of her grille.
After that, sometimes she'd start talking
all by herself, a loud deep gargling
that shook her body—limbs akimbo,
skirt inching up—showing her panties
with the MADE IN HONG KONG tag
still attached. *I HURT myself!* she cried.
Please carry me. I'm hungry. I'm sleepy.
She awoke with two black marks on her leg
and a crack on her back along the seam.
A rash of Chatty Pox dotted her cheeks.
Give me a kiss, she ordered, and I did.
I'd do anything to shut her up.

Where are we going? bratty Chatty Cathy
warbled for the last time.
She stopped wanting to play. Stopped
saying *I love you*. Next, laryngitis.
Then a growling sound.
Her O-ring cracked off, the frayed
string a strangled loop spooling
inside her damaged voice box.
Then she was mute, stiffly propped
against my bed pillow like a fancy
boudoir doll made only for show.

Danny Kaye at the Palace

He kissed me once in his dressing room
at the Palace Theater. I was six,
and he was forty, and my aunt Rozzy
had had a fling with him years before
he was famous, when he was a *tummler*
clowning at her first husband's hotel
in the Catskills. Danny Kaye was famous
in our house too. My family would talk
about his family like family; his daughter,
Dena, just my age, was like a cousin

twice removed. How many times
had I heard the one about how Danny
and Aunt Rozzy took a midnight drive
and smashed up her husband's roadster?
(No one was hurt.) There's a snapshot
of them smooching on a rustic bench,
Danny draped impishly across *her* lap,
the boss's wife, Queen of White Roe,
not the thrice-married, thrice-divorced,
childless bookkeeper she'd become.

And on whose sumptuous lap I sat,
that matinee at the Palace, although
my orchestra seat cost her one week's pay.
Here was Danny Kaye in person,
Aunt Rozzy's Danny Kaye, rattling
off the names of 54 Russian composers

in the 38 seconds of a song named "Tschaikowsky."
"Rachmaninoff, Rimsky-Korsakoff...,"
the stage so close I could see
his spit-spray dancing with the dust.

Years later came rumors that, although
he was sunny in public, in private
he was ice. He threatened to disinherit Dena
if she ever wrote a word about him.
"Not *our* Danny," my family said.
We knew him before he was famous,
right after he changed his name from
David Daniel Kaminski to Danny Kaye,
Duvideleh to his parents, double-talker,
before he was Walter Mitty, Red Nichols,

Hans Christian Andersen, the Court
Jester, Pied Piper, Inspector General,
Anatole of Paris, the Kid from Brooklyn,
we knew him before he stood in front
of a symphony orchestra and conducted
"The Flight of the Bumblebee" using
a fly swatter as his baton—when there
was still time for him to become
my uncle Danny—who kissed my left
cheek, the last and first time we met.

My Father's Shoe Trees

After giving away his Italian suits,
I couldn't find a taker for the pair
of wooden shoe trees he slipped
inside his custom-made dress shoes
imported from England. Themselves
a luxury protecting his investment,
the cedar shoe-trees kept those shoes
in shape, kept the chestnut leather
from shrinking, so you could say
they prolonged the pampered life
of his shoes, though not his own.
Every so often he would lightly sand
the wood burnished from years
of wear and oil from his fingertips,
and the lovely cedar scent returned.
Since his death, I've displayed them
on my coffee table like *objets d'art,*
keeping their provenance secret.
Is it any stranger than casting baby
shoes in bronze? When I ask a man
his size—the size of his *feet,* that is—
they're either too long or too wide.
My father's shirts fit most slender
medium-sized men; they were easy
to dispose of. But his shoe trees
continue to be a problem.
Straight out of a classic fairy tale,

like the infamous glass slippers,
they'll only fit inside the shoes
that only fit the one pair of feet
of the future prince they're fated for.

Last Words

Once the patient stops drinking liquids, he's got up to fourteen
days to live. If he takes even a sip of water, you reset the clock.

Eleven days without a drop. The rabbi
made his rounds. They stopped her
IV and her oxygen. I asked them
to please turn off the TV's live feed
to the empty hospital chapel, lens
focused on the altar and crucifix—
it seemed like the wrong God watching
over her, up there, near the ceiling.
And because hearing is the last
sense to go, the nice doctor spoke
to me in a separate room. He said
it's time to say goodbye. Next day,
he returned her to her nursing home
to die. Her nurses said just talk
to her; let her hear a familiar voice.
I jabbered to the body in the bed.
I kept repeating myself, as I'd done
on visits before, as if mirroring
her dementia. I rubbed her hand,
black as charcoal from the needles.
I talked the way a coach spurs on
a losing team. Suddenly she opened
her eyes, smiled her famous smile,
she *knew* me, and for the first time
in a year of babbling, she spoke

my name, then, in her clearest voice
said, "I love you. You look beautiful.
This is wonderful." I urged her
to sip water through a straw. Then
two cold cans of cranberry juice,
she was that thirsty. Her fingertips
pinked up like a newborn's.
I wanted the nurses to acknowledge
my miracle, to witness my devotion
although I'd been absent all spring.
They reset the clock, resumed her oxygen.
I was like God, I'd revived her. Now
I'd have to keep talking to keep her alive.

Pickwick

That dog *never* barked, not a whimper,
so it was heaven living next door
to Pickwick and his mistress, Elzbieta,
the Polish novelist on Brattle Street,
my first apartment, my first year
out of grad school. Elzbieta had escaped
the Warsaw ghetto, then worked
for the Resistance during the War.
What had I accomplished at twenty-four?
At her holiday party, tongue-tied and
outclassed, stuck in a clot of Harvard
literati, I bonded with a fellow poet
(dressed in Marimekko) who excused
herself (she needed to pee) and set
her sloshing cocktail glass on the floor.
And before anyone could stop him,
Pickwick was lapping up her martini
like water, the olive too. Then that
scruffy knee-high mutt, who'd breezed
through puppyhood without a whine,
barked—a loud rusty hinge of a bark—
which shocked us into silence, mainly
Pickwick, who, recoiling from the report,
ricocheted around the room, frantic
to see where the noise had come from.
In the short weeks that followed,
Pickwick was a regular bar mitzvah boy
belting out his Torah portion. He barked

at what normal dogs all bark at:
doorbells, strangers, sirens, thunder,
his bowl of kibble twice a day. He growled
if you took his bowl away, howled
when other dogs within earshot howled,
igniting the poodle on the second floor.
By Easter, Pickwick was barking in long,
rhythmic stanzas that kept me awake
at night. I couldn't sleep, couldn't write.
But excited dogs love to bark, and if
you yell at them to stop, they think
that you're barking right back at them,
and they only bark harder and louder,
so I didn't shout or pound on the wall,
or bother asking Elzbieta to shush him,
but suffered with earplugs until another
apartment on a different floor was free.
Like a poet finding his voice,
once Pickwick started barking,
nothing could make him stop.

Gratitude

After Mom died we all worried about him,
alone in the apartment above the store.
But every day he took a three-mile walk.
Learned to meditate. Watched what he ate.
Phoned every Sunday to report the usual.
One Sunday in March, he called, excited,
as if Perrier was running through his veins.
On his walk in the park that day a squirrel
was blocking the path right in front of him.
It had somehow gotten one of those plastic
thingamajig rings that holds a six-pack
together stuck around its neck like a yoke.
The squirrel looked as if it was asking for
help, so my father bent down and flipped
that whatchamacallit over its head
and freed it. The squirrel stood a minute
as if studying him, then scampered across
the busy traffic circle into the woods.

The next night, Monday, he called again.
Not an emergency, he was quick to say.
Today in the park he saw that cockamamie
squirrel standing directly in his path,
waiting to thank him! Was he deranged?
Maybe solitude was finally getting to him
or he needed a medication changed.
What a story, I said, but really,
how could the squirrel tell my father

from all the other walkers on the path?
By his scarf? His mustache? His smell?
And how did my father know it was
that same squirrel? Don't get too close,

I said. Next time, you could get rabies!
He was a harrowing five-hour drive away.
I could just see him on his rounds that day,
telling Kenny at the deli his new best story
and Jack the bank teller and Henry and
people at the ShopRite waiting in line
beside *National Enquirer*s and *TV Guide*s—
perfect strangers, nodding, agreeing
with him about the strangeness of life.
It's like that Aesop's fable where a slave
named Androcles removes a thorn
from a lion's paw. The moral?
"Gratitude is the sign of noble souls,
be they human or animal." That winter,
my father died. Along with everything
else about him, I miss his Sunday calls.
Gratitude's reciprocal: my father saves
a squirrel and the squirrel gives my father
a story to tell.

A Reminder

My husband gets a forwarded postcard in the mail
from Temple Beth Israel: it asks him

to light a Yahrzeit memorial candle
for his (*beloved father Larry*)
on the evening of (*January 14*)—
the blanks for name and date, in parentheses,
filled in with blue ballpoint ink.

I don't want to see my husband's face
when he reads it.
I never met my father-in-law.
He never met our daughter,
his granddaughter.

A year ago my husband flew to the funeral in Ohio.
He sat shiva at his uncle's house,
with strangers—his father's friends and business associates,
and buddies his father played poker with
every Friday night for the last twenty years.

Tomorrow's the 14th.
There's not a candle in the house.
My husband's working, out of town.
I'll have to go to the Grand Union's Jewish shelf,
where they keep the matzoh meal and kasha,
to buy a Yahrzeit candle.

His father walked out on his wife
of thirty years, stole the family savings, cleaned out
the safe-deposit box, disappeared
to another state for two decades,
his whereabouts a blank. Apparently
he found a girlfriend, a house, a job, another life.

Every morning for the last ten years,
he ate breakfast at McDonald's
with his best friend, Sol.
Sol told my husband,
"You could have knocked me over with a feather.
In the whole time I knew him,
your father never once mentioned
that he had a son."

Four sons. My husband's brothers
all written out of their father's will.

The obituary arrived a week after the funeral:
The deceased has no immediate survivors.

My husband will be home in plenty of time
to light the candle at sundown.
But he's ambivalent.
Guilty if he lights it.
Guilty if he doesn't.

American Girls

The first of the dolls she asked for
was Addy, a Negro slave escaped from the Civil War.
Addy arrived at Emma's sixth birthday party
wearing her historically accurate dress,
drawers, stockings, cap-toed boots,
and carrying a paperback copy of *Meet Addy*.
But Addy's kerchief, her "half-dime
from Uncle Solomon," her cowry shell,
her authentic Underground Railroad maps
and what the catalogue calls "the traditional
family recipe for sweet potato pudding,"
and the hardcover book—*they* cost extra.
Our daughter didn't get them, and she didn't get
the wooden hobnailed trunk to store them in.

Catalogues were coming every month now.
We didn't want to spoil her,
but on Emma's seventh birthday
a Victorian orphan joined the family:
Samantha, who'd lived in a mansion and slept
in an easy-to-assemble brass-plated four-poster bed.
Samantha let Emma remove her checked
taffeta dress, and slip her into her pink, lace-
ruffled nightgown and matching bloomers,
and tuck her into her bed—
on the floor at the foot of Emma's bed—
beside Addy's authentic rope bed,

which cost more than any *actual* Addy's *actual* bed
would have cost, if Addy'd *actually* had one.

The next morning, poring over the catalogue,
Addy and Samantha started fighting
just as real sisters do.
Fought over who should wear the Kwanzaa outfit,
who would wear the genuine sterling silver
Star-of-David necklace,
tearing each other's hair out over
the red silk Chinese pajamas, and who'd get to keep
the brass gong and pretend firecrackers
after the Chinese New Year's celebration was over.
They fought over the ballerina tutu,
hula skirt, Girl Scout uniform,
items introduced to the catalogue
when the "American Girl of Today" was born.

For her eighth birthday, Emma's father and I
custom-made ourselves a "Girl of Today."
We chose from (blonde, red, brunette, black)
(straight or kinky) hair to brush
and braid, wash and set, chose
her eye color and skin tone from the
(Hispanic-American, African-American,
Asian-American, Caucasian) models shown,
and created a brown-eyed, brown-haired,

huggable, "unique one-of-a-kind original."
Just like Emma, our own little girl.
The minute she got her new doll, Emma
named it Emma, and typed "Emma's Life Story"
on her mini make-believe Mac.

But soon Emma grew tired of "Emma,"
as she'd grown tired of her other "girls,"
leaving them on their respective beds,
where they closed their variously shaded brown eyes
and slept the half-sleep of the undead—
toys on their way to becoming heirlooms—
only to be roused for a makeshift tea party
when a younger child came to visit.
Yet I often long to play with "Emma,"
who was such good company, after all,
and who lies unkempt, ear to her "boom box,"
on the top bunk of her bunk bed.
I wish I could brush her lifelike hair,
wipe her face and dress her up again.

New catalogues keep arriving in the mail.
Though Emma has lost interest, I can't resist
paging through things to buy (*camisa, mantilla*)
for Josefina (with a Spanish *J*),
who lived on a *rancho* in New Mexico in 1824,
and comes with her own line of furniture...
I'm afraid I'll have to pass on her

and on all future "Girls of Tomorrow,"
who have yet to ride the assembly line's
long fallopian tube of Time;
the girls my daughter's daughters' daughters—
whose faces I'll never see,
whose names I can't imagine—
will carry, as I once carried mine.

Mirror/Mirror

You can't step twice into the same mirror,
said Heraclitus, of the river's mirror.

A vessel holding water was the first mirror.
A mirror held to nostrils, life's last mirror.

"Who is fairest?" the queen asked her mirror.
A vampire has no reflection in a mirror.

Those backward letters without a mirror
spell AMBULANCE in your rear-view mirror.

After Mom died, I covered all the mirrors
with cloth, sat seven days without mirrors.

Staring at myself staring in my mirror,
"I" became the "other" in the mirror.

Watching themselves making love in the mirror,
they were aroused by the couple in the mirror.

The amputee stood at an angle that mirrored
his phantom limb, now visible, mirrored.

In the *Arnolfini Wedding Portrait*'s mirror,
its painter's captive in that convex mirror.

A palindrome is another kind of mirror
like the couplets in a ghazal's mirror.

Her beloved's eyes were her only mirror.
Seven bad years when he broke a mirror.

I avoid, when I can, cruel three-way mirrors.
"Mute surfaces," Borges called mirrors.

As Vanity combs her long hair in the mirror,
an old bald skull awaits in the mirror.

Standing between two facing mirrors,
I shrank down a long hallway of mirrors.

Which Jane are you? I asked my mirror.
My mirror answered, *Ask another mirror.*

Gaslight

He points out that she fidgets and wrings her hands,
so she sits on them when he's near.

When the telephone rings and she answers,
no one's on the line.

And she doesn't remember his telling her
about the dinner party on Friday.

If he had, she would have brought her dress
to the dry cleaner. And washed her hair.

Then one Sunday, looking up a number
in his address book, she finds

a snapshot of a woman
she doesn't know. A stranger.

He says it's a bookmark.
Has no idea how it got there. Or

who this woman is, or the numbers repeated
on last month's phone bill, or why

she doesn't trust him. Like Paula—
exactly like the wife in *Gaslight*.

And isn't he her very own Charles Boyer,
the husband who calls his wife hysterical,

high-strung, absent-minded,
inclined to imagine things?

Any similarity to actual persons, living or dead,
is purely coincidental, says the disclaimer.

Staging Your House

The chandelier does not convey.
It was your mother's. You'll take it with you
when you move. But all the fixtures and fittings,
anything attached to the property, conveys.
It stays. Toilets and ceiling fans convey,
and the refrigerator dispensing crushed ice and cubes
when it's in the mood.

And when the professionals are done with it,
your house is as bland as when you first bought it,
uncluttered, impersonal as a hotel.
Your daisies replaced with a funereal bouquet.
As for the Tomato Bisque foyer—too quirky.
Now it's beige.

The creaky eleventh stair;
the leaky faucet, Muzak to your insomnia;
the Japanese maple scratching the screen;
the church bells, when you moved in,
ringing at fifteen-minute intervals, interrupting
your every thought, then you stopped hearing them;
the limos and hearses parked across the street,
drivers in dark suits smoking, waiting for the wedding
or the funeral to end—they all convey.

They say you can't take it with you, but you can.
You're not going to heaven, you're just moving.

The roofer, the gardener, the plumber,
the stonemason who cobbled a path
of flagstones to the front door,
journeymen you relied on, like family, do not convey.
The kisses, the arguments on the porch,
tears washed down the drain do not convey.
But the shutters and awnings and azaleas, pink
and darker pink, that bloomed annually without fail
on your daughter's birthday, and the gigantic
tulip poplar you were afraid a storm would uproot,
topple, crushing your neighbors' roof, killing
that nice elderly couple—they convey.

Long after the open house, the contract, the closing,
driving past the church, you find yourself,
as if in a trance, pulling into your old driveway.
The house looks the same, but different.
New shutters. New fence.
A bike tipped over on the lawn.

Where to Find Us

After you've crossed the "singing bridge,"
and passed Legare's Farm Market — fresh
pumpkins, peas, pick-your-own strawberries —
drive two more miles, give or take a tenth.

Here's where my husband always said,
"At Peck Hill Road hang a sharp left,"
and I'd add my two cents, just to irk him,
"But you're not at Peck Hill Road yet!"

I always hated it when he interrupted me
giving directions, and he hated it when
I'd point out every landmark along
the way: my woman's crow's-nest view —

not my husband's God's-eye view —
directions we bickered over for forty years.
Watch for the tilted green wooden pole.
You'll miss it. Everyone misses the turn

the first time. For a century and a half,
it was "Left at the old sugar shack,"
and people knew exactly where to turn,
until it collapsed and was dismantled,

its barn board sold as fancy wainscoting
for designer kitchens. *You* may see only

an empty space, but to *us* that shack's
still disappearing board by board.

When was the last time you saw us?
You'd have to be blind not to see
our three-story barn's rusted roof
up ahead, and our 1840s farmhouse.

Are the clapboards still white?
This house just didn't want to be painted,
it liked being naked, no matter how
many coats we'd apply, it blistered

and peeled the minute after the paint
dried. If you're not stuck behind
a swaying hay wagon or snow plow,
from Montpelier it should take you

twenty minutes, tops.
Stick to my directions, you won't get
lost. If you'd listened to my husband,
you'd be halfway to Montreal.

Though it may look like no one's home,
the mud room door is always open.
We're in the back pasture, waiting,
buried under the crabapple tree.

Rainbow Weather

First my body feels it, like hunger
or an itch prickling my entire skin,
and the light outside looks odd,
saturated, tinted greenish gold,
so I drop the spoon, or the book
I'm reading, and hurry to the back
porch, where a sun shower's busy

pelting the pasture's tall grass.
When it happens, it's always
in the late afternoon, and always
directly over the crabapple tree:
a faint shimmer that intensifies,
steeping the sky in a seven-banded
cord of color that lasts a minute,

then vanishes. Or it may loiter
a half hour—neighbors phone neighbors
to go look outside. Occasionally
it's a lucky double—the sign
that told me I was pregnant.
And because I know exactly where
it will be, I love to show it off.

I point. I wait. And it appears,
as if commanded, to an awed round
of applause. Greg Mosher, who sold us
our house, must have known,

and the Bassages before him, the Knoxes
before them, all five Peck boys
and girls, their father, and his father

before him—farmer who felled
the trees, positioned the beams,
pitched the view just so—storm clouds
scuttling away, sun warming his back,
like that first astonished witness
on his homemade ark, beholding
the covenant, the promise.

EYE LEVEL

Either the Darkness alters—
Or something in the sight
Adjusts itself to Midnight—
And Life steps almost straight.
— Emily Dickinson, 419

For my parents

Witness

Chilled moonrise, his mother now in bed,
her terror tranquilizing with the cold idea,
we scoured the neighborhood with searchlights,
the woods behind his school; the lumberyard's
cesspool, a black moon in the grass, called
everyone and no one, called to me.
Jackknifed in the pipe, he could not shinny up
the mud and ooze, the narrow walls collapsing,
dark water notching up his spine.
Did he see me swimming in the glazed eye
of light he woke to, did he wake at all,
as the icy noose of water tightened around
his chin, the north star of the squad car
flashing? Navigating by touch and shadow,
our lasso caught his feet. We tugged.
His head slipped deeper in the cavity.
Helpless, I held my breath. Hand over hand,
we hauled him up and out into the humming air:
limp and shivering, feet-first.
He swung a long moment over us, shiny,
bigger than we thought, his face bruised blue
by metallic light. Cold gravity; release.
He whined like nothing human in my arms.

The Advent Calendar

Outside the bay windows
the sky fills up with snow.
The pentangular wall of night
reflects my reading lamp
into a constellation.
But a neighbor glancing in
can see just one lamp shining.

The calendar windows
seal off a winter landscape too.
Skaters glide across a pond
over the round window in the ice.
Behind the shutters of a stall
an aproned carpenter
sweeps sawdust into a pile,
barely enough to fill a thimble.

A child peers through
the bakery window.
I slit along the window frame,
lifting the boy and glass wall of tortes
off into a prophecy...

As his window swings open
the boy sees himself
up to his elbows in flour

beside a pyramid of loaves.
Is the night wind sifting the flour?
Has a blizzard turned the kitchen
inside out?

Oh woman in the foreground
with your beautiful skirts,
do you contain a window too —
like the church's arched door
opening on a nave of tiny worshipers?
Behind the clerestory window
a crèche appears —
the Madonna mobbed by putti,
the infant cushioned
on the backs of sheep.

Madonna of the Beautiful Skirts,
you carried into Egypt
within your body
a world of such belief!
I can only carry
myself into my life.
In my windowed room, only I
am multiplied
and pray to be whole.

2

These lives I randomly
release into the world
like doves!

In seconds I do it!
I unlock the stalls,
twenty-three windows open,
all but the window of the moon.

I used to wish those numbered days
would vanish, a miracle!
But would hurrying
break the spell,
would the windows turn real
and shatter in my eyes?

Better to shut them,
keep the future out,
as this last window
of the moon stays shut.
But who can resist
the moon's bright eye
in this paper sky,
or any other?

Once, looking for the moon,
at the far end

of the telescope, I saw
the echo of my own dark eye
shining. The more I tried
to take the glass away, the more
that eye deepened into mine,
burning beyond the human shape
the self takes on.

Can light be so intense
the future's in a glance?
If I hold my hand to light,
the bright lattice of my bones
shines through.

3
Stars are falling.
I open the crescent window of the moon.
Inside, a man is hiking in sheer daylight
clear across Tibet where it is day.
The mountain peaks break in yellow waves
as the man walks unconcerned
on a tide of birds.
Morning lies behind this window,
the window of sunrise,
its movement over the world
arrives always with gifts in both arms.

A Letter Sent to Summer

Oh summer, if you would only come
with your big baskets of flowers,
dropping by like an old friend
just passing through the neighborhood!

If you came to my door disguised
as a thirsty biblical angel
I'd buy all your hairbrushes and magazines!
I'd be more hospitable
than any ancient king.

I'd personally carry your luggage in.
Your monsoons. Your squadrons of bugs.
Your plums and lovely melons.
Let the rose let out its long long sigh.
And Desire return to the hapless rabbit.

This request is also in my own behalf.
Inside my head it is always snowing,
even when I sleep. When I wake up,
and still you have not arrived,
I curl back into my blizzard of linens.

Not like winter's buckets of whitewash.
Please wallpaper my bedroom
with leafy vegetables and farms.
If you knocked right now,

I would not interfere.
Start near the window.
Start right here.

Noon

Along the creek girls are lifting
their thin skirts and as they bend
low, under their loose scoop-neck
blouses the pale flesh shows.
They notice you and wave, turn back
again laughing, dipping their feet
into the cool water. Now scarves go;
they unpin their hair. On the banks
the grass turns down like sheets
and the sun is big and close.
You can barely see them through
the heat as they peel and peel away
their clothes. And when they open
their slender arms to you, thinking
they are doing this because they
want to, thinking there is a choice,
who can blame them for giving in
this easily, or you, nearer now
to yourself than ever as they pull
you with them, sister, down.

Home Movies: 1949

Woozy from death they hog the camera
that revives them, blinking like children
we shook awake. Intensities of plaid
coagulate on screen. One distant cousin.
Above the picnic baskets, bobbing
like icebergs they investigate the silence
each time we run them through the same
embarrassing routines. I am swimming.
In the river my father's trousers cling,
two drooping cylinders. He stumbles
toward us, digs deep, retrieves a cow bone.
Thrusts it like a barbell above his head.
Soloing, my uncle handles his trombone
careful as dentures. Next to me his widow
stiffens. An aunt glides by with a thermos.
We are kept always out of earshot,
safe. Clutching their trophies they wave
us off. I forget how cold the water was.

Fortunes Pantoum

You will go on a long journey
You will have a happy and healthy life
You will recover valuables thought lost
You will marry and have many children

You will have a happy and healthy life
Your sweetheart will always be faithful
You will marry and have many children
You will have many friends when you need them

Your sweetheart will always be faithful
Soon you will come into a large inheritance
You will have many friends when you need them
You will succeed in your line of work

Soon you will come into a large inheritance
You will travel to many new places
You will succeed in your line of work
Be suspicious of well-meaning strangers

You will travel to many new places
A message from a distance is soon to be received
Be suspicious of well-meaning strangers
Important news from an unexpected source!

A message from a distance is soon to be received
You will meet a dark and handsome foreigner

Important news from an unexpected source!
Do not take unnecessary chances

You will meet a dark and handsome foreigner
You have a fear of visiting high places
Do not take unnecessary chances
Your misunderstanding will be cleared up in time

You have a fear of visiting high places
Grasp at the shadow and lose the substance
Your misunderstanding will be cleared up in time
Sometimes you worry too much about death

Grasp at the shadow and lose the substance
You will recover valuables thought lost
Sometimes you worry too much about death
You will go on a long journey

The Lifeguard

The children vault the giant carpet roll
of waves, with sharp cries swing legs
wide over water. A garden of umbrellas
blooms down the stretch of beach. Far
offshore always I can spot that same
pale thumbprint of a face going under,
grown bigger as I approach, the one arm circling,
locking rigid around my neck. The other
as its fist hooks and jabs my head away.
Ear to the conch, ear to the pillow,
beneath a canopy of bathers each night
I hear the voice and pry the jaws apart,
choke on the tangle of sable hair that blurs
the dead girl's mouth: that anarchy
of breath dog-soft and still at my neck.
She calls from the water glass I drink from.
From my own throat when I swallow.

Sounding the Lake

> This is a remarkable depth for so small an area, but not an
> inch of it can be spared in the imagination.
> —Thoreau

The one cloud
in a blue sky
is also the one cloud

in the lake, the feeling
of something
to be distrusted

that cloud
constantly
reinventing itself.

In long light
minnows move like stars
in shallow water.

Who can calculate
the light-years
from fish to fish?

You're living
your whole life
with someone

who is more
important to you
than skin.

I watch the white
boats shift
lakeside to lakeside.

But the cloud
in the lake
is more beautiful,

its shimmer,
in which I constantly
mistake myself

and fall in. This is
how it is
with you and me.

I would rather be the lake
filling the silent
yawn of the earth

where trout
move
through clear water.

I would rather be
the trout, or
the dream of the trout,

the spasm of cloud
in the trout's brain,
oh anything but this

feeling, which is
what breaks me, friend,
when you enter.

Eye Level

*If exposed to total darkness for seventy-two hours, the retina
degenerates, causing partial loss of vision.*

1. NORTH

Wisteria worked its patient violence on the house.
Working at civility, we moved
from room to room like diplomats,
dividing china, dismantling the easy chair.
Out from the linen closet, the tent collapsed
into a small bag of telescoping poles; the compass;
the Coleman stove's blue bracelet of flame.
Your Swiss Army knife tamed any emergency—
miniature corkscrew, screwdriver, fish scaler, file—
blades snapped into that miracle of steel.
I slipped it in my pocket, the red handle
shining like a deep wound in my palm. Only this
I kept to cut my narrow path away from you.

2. HAITI: SKIN DIVING

My legs break
the thick glass floor
of water.

My foot magnifies
blue as the foot
of a corpse.

One unshuttable eye
spans my face
and sees easily

what two eyes
can barely see.
I breathe

and go under.
Sea urchins fan
black sprays of quills.

Sea fans sway
at right angles
to the current.

My snorkel's ball
spins in its atmosphere
of breath

like tiny Mars
above my head.
The sixth sense

must be gravity!
I measure distance
now by fin-kicks,

the sun's angle.
Finned, the swimmer
wades backward

to the sea,
waist-deep, to plunge
and turn almost

weightless inside
the moving
body once again.

All the lyre-tailed,
stippled, rainbow-
flecked bodies

flash — shaped by water.
A school of fish
spills from the coral

and circles me.
I stiffen
without moving.

My fingertip's
slightest tremor
could shatter that order,

blurring
as my breath
clouds the mask.

3. PORT-AU-PRINCE

In the thatched *choucoune,*
I learned Creole proverbs
from the maid. *The fish*
trusts the water and in the water
it is cooked.

Was that thunder in the harbor?
Smoke funneled from the Iron Market.
The gardener shinnied up a palm tree
like a sailor up a mast,
binoculars bouncing against his back.
The maid translated his shouts
half in Creole, half in French,
and still I could not connect.
I telephoned the Embassy—
heard, fractured by static,
"…an old military plane
crashed in the street,
skidding into a *tap-tap*
jammed with passengers."

When the hawk strikes,
if he doesn't take feathers
he takes straw.

All varieties of blood
bloom at eye level. *Flamboyant.*
Belle Mexicaine. Acres of poinsettia
flame up the cliffs
along the Kenscoff Road.

The last hurricane
cut the banana plantation down.
The way an image
inverts inside the eye,
bunches of bananas jutted
like chandeliers out of the ground.
The palace leveled by jungle,
accessible only by air.
Violence civilized
by machete, jeep, and climate.

4. BLACKOUT

Only the knife knows
what is in the heart
of the yam.

A blazing eye
will not set the house
on fire.

All electric power out;
I swung the shutters
open and leaned

over the fretwork
of the balcony,
as the city

sank—tier
by brilliant tier—
into the harbor.

Stumbling toward
the door, my fingers
skimmed the Braille plaster

of the walls, until
my bare feet
felt the landing,

the wooden boxes
of the steps.
In my hand,

my butane lighter
slid a small circle
down the stairs,

and the stairs
became all motion,
surfaces angled

off to surfaces
I couldn't see;
and I, suddenly

brave among shadows,
yelled out
to scare the maid,

"Esprit! Esprit!"
thinking it meant
ghost...

*Save yourself
from drowning.
The day a leaf*

*falls in the water
may not be
the day it sinks.*

5. NORTH: THE FISH

The blind and depigmented fish Amblyopsis
spelaea *inhabits streams in the dark zones of
caves in southern Indiana.*

In the laboratory, the scientist
explains what I am about to see.
How, in Huddelson's cornfield,
the farmer discovered the cave
when his pig fell in the hole.
Lowered by rope into a twilit chamber,
the scientist landed on a dirt mound
studded with lost things: a hoe, twisted
vertebrae, keys, shreds of tinfoil—
whatever shiny caught the pack rats' eyes.

The scientist shuts off the lights
and guides me one step up, unbolting
a room of cold and dark so dense
its clarity shocks instantly—
as in the nightmare dive, the dreamer
wakes midair over water.
In the frozen halo of my iris,
the dark target widens.

Total darkness isn't black,
but is a deep and pit-like gray
that draws the eye into its depths.

The scientist passes me the flashlight
like a cigarette. Each fish
looks like a finger's length of quartz.
The colorless scales have the sheen
of silk, silver mesh around the gills.
The fins, thin undulant fans, quiver.
Cut one open, its blood runs clear as water.
Light shines straight through its head.
I focus on where the eyes should be.
Skin stretches unbroken over the skull,
flat and smooth as a thumbnail.
Eye sockets, shadows trapped in ice.

I dip my hand into the water
to touch the glacial head.
The fish darts away!
It stuns like current as I jerk back,
my hand rigid at my side.
My eye burns beyond its chemicals.

6.
Across the garden
two birds call
into my sleep.

What was it
I was dreaming?
—a mermaid turning

in your net
you wished to make
human by an act

of love? Landlocked,
I was only
divided by desire.

In sleep,
when each has lost
the enterprise of

self, and the heart
no longer steers
within the body's

limits, then
sun, moon, and skull
are equal in the mind.

On a seabed, or bed
of linen, the same
skeletal thrash

in darkness,
choking on water
as on air.

Desire's
just the interval
in birdsong.

The two call
across the distance
of the bed.

The voices call
despite weather
or temperament.

I let you go.
But see how my desire
drew you in.

7. *TROMPE L'OEIL*

Tonight, the grid
of trolley wires
that canopies the street

sags under
the sky's dark weight.
I glanced out

the window the moment
the trolley passed—
spattering an enormous

blue-white spark
that filled my bedroom
like pistol shot—

branding trees,
the house opposite,
where still cars

bloomed in points
of light. Surveying
the injury, I focused

on the dark.
Trees uprooted, cars
parked in air.

Everywhere I looked
their outlines
shocked the dark

and floated exactly
as they were:
double-exposed on

the ceiling, the wall,
burning the back
of my hand.

Was I looking
at tomorrow, daylight
out of any time,

or history
repeating itself
in waves?

In seconds,
the image began
to fade.

What the eye cannot
hold, it holds
and sharpens

in memory, when
a detail overlooked
ignites

on the white periphery.
The glitter of
things outside

short-circuit
beyond sight.
The spark deepens

in the brain
as the dark grows
more intense,

when, for an instant,
light is all
that's permanent.

THE MINUTE HAND

Even while we speak, the hour passes.
—Ovid

For Howard

A Clock

Summer twilight tamps down the farmhouse roof.
Kneeling in his lettuce patch, the farmer
stares through the wrought-iron bars of the III,
a rusting harp that heaven plunked down
beside him, junk too heavy to haul away.
He squints at his wife beyond the IX,
tending even rows of greens.
Rising and falling between them,
the steady hands of the Planter's Clock
skim the white enamel dial
that time has turned to cream.

The sun dips and disappears
as the moon rises over the minute hand.
The pageant glides by, on gears.
Up in thinner air where the moon aspires,
a cornucopia spills stars and ripening planets—
a tomato Mars, a turnip Saturn, and four
greenbean comets whipping their tails.
A gigantic ear of corn
floats like a spaceship over the barn.

Rooted in the ticking rim of earth,
the farmer and his wife can never touch.
Bright as the moon, an onion sheds its light
on their awestruck faces morning, noon, and night.
If only she could slip inside
her pretty trapezoid of home

and cook her husband a good square meal,
but the farmhouse door is painted shut,
the curtains drawn—
hiding the feather bed, the empty crib,
the cupboard filled with loaves of bread.

High in that harvested astronomy,
the onion is incapable of tears.
Whatever Intelligence placed it
like a highlight shining in the farm wife's eye
also chiseled the lists into the bedrock
of planting charts on which she stands—
tables of days and months and seasons,
killing frosts, auspicious times to sow—
indelible as the stone tablets of the Law.

The farm wife casts her vision higher even
than the moving parts of heaven.
Do other worlds like hers exist
in rooms in distant galaxies—
exact copies of her farm with weathervane,
weathered barn, and a husband
on his knees, weeding or praying,
his face a wrinkled thumbprint?

It's like opening a familiar book:
the illustration always stays the same
no matter what time of day she looks.

The same furrows stitch the fields;
and haystacks, heaps of golden needles,
dot the farthest pastures, the last of which
drops neatly into the horizon's ditch.
Dig potatoes now. Thin the beets.
It's five to nine. Years later than she thinks.
She feels the earthquake each minute makes
behind that shaking scenery,
heartbeats coming from so far away
she has to cup her ears to hear them.

Pharaoh

So as not to be lonely
in the afterlife
the boy-king was buried
with his most cherished things

items he would need
on his journey—
toys, enough food
for a lifetime, maybe more

a golden cage
on whose perch
his canary
still sings like a rusty hinge

his throne
his cup
a spoon or two
made of solid gold

urns filled with oil
urns filled with honey
some broken dishes
plenty of wine

his gold mask
a perfect likeness

on which his highness
crayoned a faint mustache

his silk tunic
a supply of papyrus
an ivory comb
with no missing teeth

a mirror on which
to breathe a cloud—
the tomb's only weather
that, and dust

his dog
a golden ball
two old servants
curled at his feet

under the bandages
pharaoh, a boy,
buried with his hands
in his pockets

a star chart
carved on the ceiling
under which
a deep healing is taking place

Young Woman on the Flying Trapeze

Shooting with his Bolex,
my father kept nature in perspective.
He caught the trapeze artist catching
his partner in midair, swinging

in and out of my line of sight.
I was five. In nightmares, the body
falls straight into the dreamer's eye;
he wakes before hitting bottom.

Did I blink then, did I glance away,
the moment that she tumbled
like an angel out of heaven?
I don't remember, but I saw her fall.

My father slows the projector down
frame by frame; the trapeze artist
aims for her partner, and somersaults.
Her partner's wavering hand

connects with her sequined wrist;
but his other hand misses, clamping
shut on the air that frames her,
no connection, her body blurring

its slurred speech, as scanning
the sawdust floor, the camera locates

the broken italic of her flesh.
No connection! I can't remember

no matter how many times I see her,
no matter how many times
my father runs the film.
Projecting in reverse, he has her

climb the ladder of light
one more time, for my benefit,
but he can't rescue her
from gravity forever.

Backward, she bullets up toward
the bull's-eye of her partner's fist,
her face enlarged in its unknowing—
and lands back on the platform,

squarely on her own two feet!
Spliced into the same reel, unreal
documents of the commonplace.
A picnic under way. Then it is Sunday.

The living room upholstery is brand new.
The Frigidaire is white-enamel white.
Then, a lucky break to catch this,
I am crawling, hoisting myself up

my mother's skirts to take my first
steps, fighting to keep my balance,
staggering toward whatever it was
I reached for out of the camera frame—

held and lost in that drifting
instant of attention,
from which the body performs
its miraculous escape.

The Russian Doll

After Elder Olson

Six inches tall, the Russian doll
stands like a wooden bowling pin.
The red babushka on her painted head
melts into her shawl and scarlet
peasant dress, and spreading over that,
the creamy lacquer of her apron.
A hairline crack fractures the equator
of her copious belly,
that when twisted and pulled apart,
reveals a second doll inside,
exactly like her, but smaller,
with a blue babushka and matching dress.
An identical crack circles her middle.

Did Fabergé fashion a doll like her
for a czar's daughter? Hers would be
more elaborate, of course, and not a toy—
emerald eyes, twenty-four-karat hair,
and with filigreed petticoats
like a chanterelle's gills blown inside out.
An almost invisible fault line
would undermine her waist,
and a platinum button that springs her body open.

Now I have two dolls: mother and daughter.
Inside the daughter, a third doll is waiting.

She has the same face,
the same figure,
the same fault she can't seem to correct.
Inside her solitary shell
where her duplicate selves are breathing,
she can't be sure
whose heart is beating, whose ears
are hearing her own heart beat.

Each doll breaks into
a northern and a southern hemisphere.
I line them up in descending order,
careful to match each womb
with the proper head—a clean split,
for once, between the body and the mind.
A fourth head rises over the rim
of the third doll's waist,
an egg cup in which her descendants grow
in concentric circles.

Until last, at last, the two littlest dolls,
too wobbly to stand upright,
are cradled in her cavity as if waiting to be born.
Like two dried beans, they rattle inside her,
twin faces painted in cruder detail,
bearing the family resemblance
and the same unmistakable design.

The line of succession stops here.
I can pluck them from her belly like a surgeon,
thus making the choice between fullness
and emptiness; the way our planet itself
is rooted in repetitions, formal reductions,
the whole and its fractions.
Generations of women emptying themselves
like one-celled animals; each reproducing,
apparently, without a mate.

I thought the first, the largest, doll
contained nothing but herself,
but I was wrong.
I assumed that she was young
because I could not read her face.
Is she the oldest in this matriarchy—
holding within her hollow each daughter's
daughter? Or the youngest—

carrying the embryo of the old woman
she will become? Is she an onion
all the way through? Maybe,
like memory shedding its skin,
she remembers all the way back to when

her body broke open for the first time,
to the child of twelve who fits inside her still;

who has yet to discover that self,
always hidden, who grows and shrinks,
who multiplies and divides.

Anthony

Your absent name at roll call was more present
than you ever were, forever
on parole in the back of the class.
The first morning you were gone,
we practiced penmanship to keep our minds
off you. My fist
uncoiled chains of connecting circles,
oscilloscopic hills,
my carved-up desk as rippled as a washboard.

A train cut you in half in the Jersey marshes.
You played there after school.
I thought of you and felt afraid.
One awkward *a* multiplied into a fence
running across the page.
I copied out two rows of *b*'s.
The caboose of the last *d* ran smack against
the margin. Nobody even liked you!
My *e*'s and *f*'s traveled over the snowy landscape
on parallel tracks—faint blue guidelines
that kept our letters even.

The magician sawed his wife in half,
then passed his hand through the gulf of air
where her waist should be.
Divided into two boxes, she turned and smiled
and all her ten toes flexed.

I skipped a line.
I dotted the disconnected body of each *i*.

At the bottom of the page,
I wrote your name. And erased it.
Wrote it, and erased again.

Thumbelina

Thumbelina, poor sleeping child,
swaying in the hammock of a leaf,
nested in my left hand the whole
summer of my seventh year,
her skull just the size of my thumbnail,
her bird heart ticking against my pulse.
Only a child, I was an only child,
small for my age, but a giant
towering over a clump of crabgrass.
A belly button in the dirt,
the anthill was the slave plantation
I oversaw, ants laboring
in the fork-raked furrows,
hoisting heavy sacks of cotton—
crumbs twenty times their body weight.
To be a giant, you must learn to step
softly, carefully, so as not to hurt
the working earth.
That year in school I was learning
how to add. The backyard thundered
with my mother's yelling. "Ssh.
Don't wake the sleeping Thumbelina,"
I'd whisper into my left hand.
"Don't hurt the sleeping child,"
the shell of my left hand echoed.
At home I was learning to tell time.
Each night when I tried to sleep,
I heard the alarm clock's jeweled

movement, seventeen diamond planets
on sawtooth wheels orbiting a ruby sun.
But something else was ticking
in another part of the Milky Way.
A cloud-spasm in the utter darkness,
something else was swimming into the galaxy.
Who could imagine anything as silly
as a child the size of a thumb,
a replica, a shrunken opposite,
a speck of sand that no amount
of wishing could dislodge.
Inside my mother's body, a baby
as big as a lima bean
was growing. But the child I carried
with me, who slept the sleep
of a speechless animal,
I carried for my own protection.
I never raised a hand against my mother
because the hand can crush what it protects.

High Holy Days

It was hot. A size too large,
my wool winter suit scratched.
Indian summer flaring up through fall.
The shul's broken window bled sunlight
on the congregation; the Red Sea
of carpet parted the women from the men.
Mother next to daughter, father next to son,
flipped through prayer books in unison
trying to keep the place. Across the aisle,
my father wore a borrowed prayer shawl.
A black yarmulke covered his bald spot.

The rabbi unlocked the ark
and slid the curtain open. Propped inside,
two scrolls of the Torah dressed like matching dolls,
each a king and a queen. Ribbons hung down
from their alabaster satin jackets;
each one wore two silver crowns.
I wondered, could the ancient kings
have been so small? So small,
and still have vanquished our enemies?

The cantor's voice rose
like smoke over a sacrificial altar,
and lambs, we rose to echo the refrain.
Each time we sat down
my mother rearranged her skirt.

Each time we stood up
my head hurt from the heat, dizzy
from tripping over the alphabet's
black spikes and lyres,
stick-figure battalions marching to defend
the Second Temple of Jerusalem.

Rocking on their heels, boats
anchored in the harbor of devotion,
the temple elders davened Kaddish, mourning the dead.
Our neighbor who owned the laundry down the street
covered his left wrist out of habit—
numbers indelible as those
he inked on my father's shirt collars.
Once, I saw that whole arm disappear
into a tub of soapy shirts,
rainbowed, buoyant as the pastel clouds

in *The Illustrated Children's Bible,*
where God's enormous hand reached down
and stopped a heathen army in its tracks.
But on the white-hot desert of the page
I was reading, it was noon,
the marching letters swam, the regiments
wavered in the heat,
a red rain falling on their ranks.
I watched it fall one drop at a time.

I felt faint. And breathed out sharply,
my nose spattering blood across the page.

I watched it fall, and thought,
You are a Chosen One,
the child to lead your tribe.
I looked around the swaying room.
Why would God choose me
to lead this congregation of mostly strangers,
defend them against the broken windows,
the spray-painted writing on the walls?

Overhead, the everlasting light, a red bulb,
was burning. As if God held me in His fist,
I stumbled down the synagogue stairs
just in time to hear
a cyclone of breath twist through
the shofar, a battle cry so powerful
it blasted city walls to rubble.
I reeled home through the dazed traffic
of the business day—
past shoppers, past my school,
in session as usual,
spat like Jonah from the whale
back into the Jew-hating world.

The Game of Jackstraws

One at a time from the pile
each player in turn tries

to remove the jackstraws—
the miniature hoes, shovels,

ladders, pickaxes, rakes—
without moving any of the others.

Light as a bird bone,
the fragile sword fallen free

from your lucky scatter
is easily yours.

You may keep it and attempt
another. Using the tiny hook

or your fingers, you barely
touch a wrench when the hammer

below it stirs.
On your next turn, careful

as a paleontologist,
bones craning over bones,

you lift a pitchfork
cantilevered on a scythe

balanced on the flat blade
of an oar which rests

against the nervous edge
of the saw—one body

touching the body of another
which has touched another's

body, and so on, that graveyard
of relations better left buried

and forgotten like the casual love
you fall out of and out of.

The more chances you are given,
the more the diminishing returns.

If you had the hammer
you could fix the stairs

that lead to the basement
that shelters the rat

that shows you his nest
where the nails are hidden.

Though your heap of jackstraws
keeps growing, the player

with the most points wins.
Why is an arrow

worth less than a saw,
and a saw worth more than a hammer?

It's a foolish carpenter
who doesn't know the value

of his tools.
The pile dwindles to two.

You'll play until love
either kills or heals you—

like the young husband
who, at daybreak, extracts himself

from his sleeping bride,
careful not to wake her,

lifting his trembling body,
pale and weightless as straw.

Tender Acre

As you slept, your pulse
flickering on your neck like a trick of light,
I thought how, earlier, beside the sleeping shape
Adam labored the whole night to stay awake,
afraid she'd vanish in the morning with the moon.
Out from the earth sprang the planet's
blurred, unpredictable life.
The pulse of the near hill—
or was it the shudder he was born with?—
rocked him. The animals, also,
that yesterday brushed like wind against his body,
were now given form. On a branch,
an icicle began to melt.
It hung, glistening and patient,
while a zipper of vertebrae inched all the way down
its back. Then bands of bargello
stitched the skin—tiny sawtooth flames
of dull gold and rust, rust and gold.
This he named *snake*.
On the topmost branch of the tree,
a bird bristled with little white thorns.
Then each thorn fanned out like a palm frond
and the bird flew away.
All day, Adam watched and listened,
but he couldn't name his loneliness—
the long "oh" of sorrow, the "ooh" of hallelujah.
Eleven curved knife blades
of his rib cage, and the twelfth

that cut his flesh without injury,
he accepted, as he accepts
these other gifts placed before him.

All night, he memorized her human shape,
so that later, were she not there,
his memory could reconstruct that absent body
from the air, and wrench him from his solitude
before the tender acre cradled her.

Wood

At eight o'clock we woke to the chain saw.
Stands of pines quivered
as the empty flatbed lumbered by
printing snakeskins on the snowy road.
The telephone company was thinning out the woods.

That afternoon, we snowshoed to a neighbor's farm.
They were gone, but their brown cow leisurely chewed
the rags of grass beneath the snow.
The sound her teeth made tearing
was like a seamstress ripping out a seam.
The enormous head swayed and dipped—
it scared us too. A skein of spittle
dangled from her lower jaw;
her tongue was big as a boot, awkward and dull pink;
her black leather nostrils snorted
a storm of cumuli, hot and white.

It got colder. Dusk held the trees in amber—
the ones, that is, left standing.
Around the fresh-cut stumps, sawdust, a fringe of twigs
were mashed into the snow.
The telephone company had cut down a tree
to erect, in its place, a sort of monument to a tree—
an imported, pitch-stuck pole with its own tin badge and number
linking house to house and voice to voice.

That night when we fed the fire, the embers
glowed under the logs the flames systematically ate,
nibbling slowly, deliberately,
from left to right. Like reading.
Sometimes, a fire devours a book all at once
in one sitting; or slowly, disinterestedly, leafs through it,
turning its pages to ash one by one.

There's pleasure in watching it ignite
and flare, pleasure that does not want to stop —
in looking around the room
and throwing in anything that will burn.
A paper napkin thrills the flame,
but briefly; a chair causes greater excitement —
its rush seat a catherine wheel sputtering, shooting sparks.
                    And punching a hole in plaster
and snapping the laths ribbing the walls;
and peeling shingles from the gray
bird wings of the roof
until the whole house burns with pleasure.
Then the fire died down. We closed the book.
A few of the ashes' soft feathers
drifted lazily up the chimney shaft
into the vanished daylight.

Persian Miniature

Two hairs plucked from the chest of a baby squirrel—
the brush of the miniaturist freezes an entire population.
Within each quarter inch,
a dozen flowers puncture the spongy ground,
and even the holes where tent poles stuck
bear ornamental weeds.
Upon a wooden balance beam—this painting's equator—
a cat is prancing.
Other animals are eating or being milked:
three spotted goats, a suede camel,
half a donkey's face lost in an embroidered feedbag.
Under a canopy, seven elders in pajamas radiate
like spokes around a bridegroom;
white beards frost the elders' chins.
Outside, a fat iron cauldron squats upon a fire
whose flames spike up golden minarets.
A kneeling boy pours coffee;
his pitcher handle, the size of a human eyelash,
is larger than the bridegroom's mustache.
A wedding! Is the bride asleep somewhere?
The bride's attendants hover in tiers
like angels in heaven's scaffolding,
but heaven, here, is the hanging gardens,
or maybe tent poles are holding heaven up.
Lappets of a tent fold back
on a woman holding her soft triangular breast
to an infant's mouth. The rug she sits on
flaps straight up behind her, like wallpaper.

One-sixteenth of an inch away,
a ram is tethered to the picture frame,
but where's the bride going to fit?
In the left-hand corner of the painting,
across what little of the sky remains,
two geese fly in tandem, pulling two wheels,
two mechanical knotted clouds.
Maybe they are pulling a storm behind them.
Crouched, swirling above the human event,
if the storm fits, it could ruin everything—
smash up the whole abbreviated acre,
flush the bride from sleep—
while the bridegroom sweeps it all away
and enters her innocent tent like thunder,
shattering the distance he's had to keep.

The Glass Slipper

The little hand was on the eight.
It scoured Cinderella's face, radiant
since her apotheosis; blue dress,
blonde pageboy curled like icing on a cake.
The wristwatch came packed in a glass slipper—
really plastic, but it looked like glass—
like one of my mother's shoes, but smaller.
High transparent heel, clear shank and sole,
it looked just big enough to fit me.

I stuffed my left foot halfway in,
as far as it would go.
But when I limped across the bedroom rug,
the slipper cut its outline
into my swelling heel.
No matter which foot I tried,
I couldn't fit the ideal
that marks the wearer's virtue,
so I went about my business
of being good. If I was good enough,
in time the shoe might fit.
I cleaned my room, then polished
the forepaws of the Georgian chair;
while in the kitchen, squirming in her highchair,
a bald and wizened empress on her throne,
my baby sister howled one red vowel
over and over.

Beside the white mulch of their chenille bedspread,
my parents' Baby Ben wind-up alarm
was three minutes off.
Each night, its moon face,
a luminous and mortuary green,
guided me between my parents' sleeping forms
where I slept
until the mechanism of my sister's hunger,
accurate as quartz,
woke my mother and me moments before
the alarm clock sprang my father to the sink
and out the door.

Seven forty-five. His orange Mercury
cut a wake of gravel in the driveway.
Like a Chinese bride I hobbled after him,
nursing my sore foot in a cotton sock.
Cinderella's oldest sister lopped off
her own big toe with a kitchen knife
to make the slipper fit, and her middle sister
sliced her heel down to size.
The dumbstruck Prince failed to notice,
while ferrying to the palace
each false fiancée,
the blood filling the glass slipper.
The shoehorn's silver tongue
consoled each one in turn,
"When *you* are Queen, you won't *need* to walk."

Dresses

After Rilke's "Some Reflections on Dolls"

On wire hangers, on iron shoulders,
the dresses float in limbo,

flat-chested spinsters who will
not dance. It is night,

the hands of the clock circle
their twelve black mountains,

upstairs the children are dreaming,
and over his red and black inks

the father figures the books,
the store as dark

as the inside of the safe.
Blouses like airy armor, trousers

that marched off the cutting table
through the needle's eye.

Dresses, it is your nature
to be possessed. With feverish hands,

your jailer will free you, undo
the two pearl buttons on your cuff

while her lover hitches up your skirt,
his rough wool against your silk . . .

eventually those caresses will wear
you away. One day you will be

the crushed body in the ragbag,
the purple in the pauper's closet,

the hand-me-down passed from one sister
to another in a distant state.

Your pockets will fill with her
perfume, ticket stubs, loose tobacco,

the telegram that changes everything
the moment it is read, and memory

makes you too painful to wear.
Houndstooth, black-watch plaid,

mauve, teal, hunter green; shades
flaring and dying with the seasons—

but not for the mannequins heaped
in the cellar under the store.

Rashes of plaster dust cover
the gash where the wrist screws

into the arm; modestly dusting,
like talcum, the chipped torsos,

bald heads, bald crotches,
and around each beautiful eye

the corona of ten spiked lashes.
In the morning, the older daughter

descends the fourteen stairs
to the store and tries on

the frothy, white organza strapless,
dragging its hem like a tide

across the fitting room floor.
And there you are in the mirror,

up to your old tricks.
She'll curtsy for her adoring father,

while her mother—
mouth bristling with straight pins—

kneels at her feet. The cash register
resumes its noisy music, browsers

breeze in and out of the swinging
door. Sooner or later, each of you

will attract your customer.
Not on your own volition will you

enter the blazing street and pass
the sister whose smooth back

you pressed against so long ago.
Not on your own volition

will you dance at a daughter's wedding,
dance unwearyingly until dawn

with energies not your own.
Nor for beauty's sake alone will you

be chosen from among all the others,
when, in severe folds, you will outwear

the body that entered your body willingly
once, and lost herself there.

A Luna Moth

For Elizabeth Bishop

For six days and nights
a luna moth, pale green,
pinned herself to the sliding screen—
a prize specimen in a lepidopterist's dream.

Tuesday's wind knocked her off the deck.
She tacked herself back up again.
During Wednesday's rain she disappeared
and reappeared on Thursday
to meditate and sun herself,
recharging her dreams from dawn to dusk,
and all night draining the current from
the deck's electric lantern.

A kimono just wider than my hand,
her two pairs of flattened wings were pale
gray-green panels of the sheerest crêpe de Chine.
Embroidered on each sleeve, a drowsing eye
appeared to watch the pair of eyes
on the wings below quite wide awake.
But they're *all* fake.
Nature's *trompe l'oeil* gives the luna
eyes of a creature twice her size.

The head was covered with snow-white fur.
Once, I got so close

it rippled when I breathed on her.
She held herself so still,
she looked dead. I stroked
the hem of her long, sweeping tail;
her wings dosed my fingers with a green-gold dust.
I touched her feathery antennae.
She twitched and calmly
reattached herself a quarter inch west,
tuning into the valley miles away
a moment-by-moment weather report
broadcast by a compatriot,
catching the scent of a purely
sexual call; hearing sounds
I never hear, having
the more primitive ear.

Serene
in the middle of the screen,
she ruled the grid of her domain
oblivious to her collected kin—
the homely brown varieties of moth
tranced-out and immobile,
or madly fanning their paper wings,
bashing their brains out on the bulb.
Surrounded by her dull-witted cousins,
she is herself a sort of bulb,
and Beauty is a kind of brilliance,

burning self-absorbed, giving little,
indifferent as a reflecting moon.

Clinging to the screen despite my comings
and goings, she never seemed to mind the ride.
At night, when I slid the glass door shut,
I liked to think I introduced her
to her perfect match
hatched from an illusion —
like something out of the Brothers Grimm —
who, mirroring her dreamy stillness,
pining for a long-lost twin,
regarded her exactly as she regarded him.

This morning,
a weekend guest sunbathing on the deck,
sun-blind, thought the wind had blown
a five-dollar bill against the screen.
He grabbed the luna, gasped,
and flung her to the ground.
She lay a long moment in the grass,
then fluttered slowly to the edge of the woods
where, sometimes at dawn,
deer nibble the wild raspberry bushes.

The Island

On one side, a series of marshes.
On the other, the ocean level as a skillet.
Across the bay, the wooden church
suffers under the weight of its weathered circumflex,
beneath which, every Sunday, the natives come to pray,
and every Tuesday, hold town meetings.
And once, when the movie people sent a scout
who wanted to rent the island,
they threw him out. He ferried back that very day.

The latticework on each widow's walk,
like the cable knitted into each fisherman's sweater,
is as individual as his thumbprint.
Summer bungalows look like pairs of scuffed brown oxfords
that hiked to sea from far inland,
stopping short at the harbor.
Mornings, tennis balls
crisscross the Common like tropical birds.
Back and forth they fly, fat, chartreuse, echoing
across this roofless aviary.
Occasional tracks of baby strollers
struggle up clay cliffs irregular as molars.
Some dunes are now off limits, like the Parthenon.
The commissioners would like to bulldoze
the whole community of nudists,
who, by noon, in most weathers,
expose their white triangles and stripes
and look like negatives of themselves.

Puckered beer cans stud the public beaches, and here and there
an evicted hermit crab bleaches.

This morning, a Spanish freighter almost sideswiped
the island's cliffs. The sailors were friendly.
They waved T-shirts from the upper decks
as if hoisting up a patchwork rainbow,
and maneuvered through the channel, blowing kisses.
We watched the ship get smaller and smaller
(almost colliding with a rust-pocked trawler),
small enough to squeeze through the neck of a bottle,
and then the horizon swallowed it.

I unfurled my towel, and read, and slept awhile
(the water was too cold to swim),
and wondered about the glass armada
bobbing along the coast's two-hundred-mile limit.
At high tide, a bottle detached itself,
and riding the assembly line of waves,
tumbled up the beach faster, faster,
landing six inches from my sunburned feet.
I held the bottle up to light—
a dozen highlights oiled the glass—
and saw a five-masted warship, uncollapsed,
with its antique mizzens still intact.

Crawling like an ant along the hull,
the ship's unlucky stowaway tried to shout,

but the plug was stuck in the bottle's throat.
Upon the pages of the sails
he'd scrawled his message in letters the bottle magnified,
gigantic as a billboard painter's:
Each night, I dream that I walk the plank
of my wife's long hair, but I can't drown.
And now, I've sailed right into your own two hands.
I've survived my island of a shipwreck.
Someday, from your shipwreck of an island,
I will rescue you.

MUSIC MINUS ONE

The writer needs an address,
very badly needs an address—
that is his roots.

—Isaac Bashevis Singer

In memory of my parents,
Essie Shore (1915–1991)
and George Shore (1915–1993)

Washing the Streets of Holland

When I was twelve, I read *The Diary of Anne Frank*.
I identified with her having to live
stories above a busy street
over a business, and having to keep quiet
for hours at a time.
I'd pad about on tiptoe,
trying not to disturb the customers
shopping in my parents' dress store below,
voices drifting up through the floorboards.
I'd pretend I was eavesdropping
from Anne's attic, while downstairs,
life went on without me.

That winter a frozen pipe cracked,
thawed, flooding the cellar under the store.
Broken mannequins lay in heaps
and rats scuttled up through the drain.
My old books, old dolls, stuffed animals
bobbed among the giant torsos.

When the water receded,
I dredged up a china plate,
sole survivor of the Blue Willow tea set
I had when I was six:
its boat and bridge and willow plumes,
its turtledoves hovering above a pagoda roof,
glazed the same delft blue as the windmills
on our tile hot plate made in Holland.

My family admired the Dutch people;
they'd hidden Jews in their houses during the War.
Once, while I was playing with my tea set,
I heard my aunt Roz say that exact thing:
"The Dutch hid Jews during the War."
My aunts and uncles sat in the living room
arguing the Holocaust—the inevitable subject—
who had helped and who had not.
Our German cleaning lady,
Mrs. Herman—my mother liked her—
literally scrubbed her way past,
on hands and knees, dragging her pail and rags.
My aunt Lil said something in Yiddish.
"What did you say?" I begged her.
Mrs. Herman had just rolled up the oval rug.

My aunt said, "Germans were bad. The Dutch were good."
"And the streets in Holland are immaculate,"
my mother said, "because every morning
the Dutch wash their sidewalks down."

And so I made up a game I called
Washing the Streets of Holland.
During my bath I'd climb out of the tub
and sprinkle Old Dutch Cleanser on the floor.
I'd hold my breath, careful
not to inhale the deadly powder.
The Dutch Cleanser lady wore a bonnet

whose flaps completely hid her face.
In her clogs and blue skirts and clean white apron,
and with a raised stick, about to strike,
she was chasing something—or someone—
on the other side of the can.
Chases Dirt, the label said.

Naked, on my hands and knees,
I'd scrub the floor with a washcloth
until my bathwater turned cold.
There was a lot of dirt in Holland,
but I was doing my part to help.
One night, my father yelled from behind the door,
"What are you doing in there?"
I was washing the streets of Holland.

Blue woman on the powder can,
blue willowware plate,
gentle brushstrokes of the pagoda roof,
blades of windmills, glazed waters of the lagoon,
blue tattoo inked in flesh,
blue ink in a diary,
blue ocean whose water is really colorless, like tears,
a flood of tears, all seven seas running together—
blurring the words
and washing them away.

Monday

My father sways before the mirror
in the blue-tiled bathroom, shaving.
The wide legs of his boxer shorts
empty as windsocks,
the neck of his white cotton undershirt
fringed with curly black hairs.

Overnight his shaving brush
has stiffened into the shape of a flame.
When he swirls it around in the mug,
the bristles plump up with lather,
as if he's folding egg whites into batter.

The empty razor lies open-jawed
in a puddle of milky water.
The double-edged blades come packed
in envelopes of five, each blade
wrapped separately in waxed paper
like a stick of gum.

My father glances at the mirror
like a woman applying makeup,
then paints on a mustache and beard
leaving only a thin mouth hole.
His lips look redder against the foam.
He lathers his chin, his Adam's apple,
the pebbly skin of his throat.

Scraping, he works quickly, in silence,
in distracted concentration,
the same way he eats his dinner every night.
But what is making my mild father so angry,
arguing with the man on the glass?
He stretches his lips into the widest
possible smile, then bares
his teeth in a grimace.

He nicks himself. Here and there,
the lather is flecked with threads of blood.
Then stroke by stroke, my father's face
gradually returns to him,
so raw and tender I ache to touch.
What in the world would harm him now,
looking as he does, with shreds
of toilet tissue stuck on his face like feathers,
each one glued with a small red dot.

Learning to Read

"Jane lived in a big white house
with a garden and a yard
and an apple tree out back."
Waiting my turn to read

out loud before the class,
my wooden desk and chair
bolted to the wooden floor,
Jane skipped and jumped and ran.

Jane—my very name—
was all we had in common.
Jane's mother knitted socks.
Mine couldn't knit a stitch.

Jane and Dick—her brother—
a matched pair
of salt and pepper shakers,
ate dinner

opposite each other,
Father facing Mother.
Two parents, two children, two pets.
My sister wasn't born yet.

Big *A* and little *a*,
upper- and lower-case *b*,

the sibling alphabet
paraded across the chalkboard

white on black, a negative
of my primer's printed page—
the page I'd read at home,
the passage I knew by heart—

where the kitten, Puff,
jumps into the sewing basket,
bats her paw and chases
a rolling ball of yarn

across the kitchen floor
and gets all tangled up.
Who'd be the lucky one
to read it to the class?

A dozen hands shot up
except Lucille's, and mine.
Shiny straight black hair,
black patent Mary Janes,

pink cat's-eye frames
studded with rhinestones—
Lucille was special.
She couldn't read or spell.

She'd had to repeat
the first grade twice,
but received straight A's
for perfect attendance.

She sat in the first row,
close to the erased blackboard,
a swirling Milky Way.
The teacher skipped Lucille

and called out, "Jane!"
I snapped back to my book,
the kitten, the sewing basket
and ball of yarn.

I opened my mouth to read
the page Fate gave to me.
Not wanting to show off,
I stumbled—on purpose—

on the words *I knew* I knew,
and got all tangled up
in that rolling ball of yarn,
unraveling its line

of looping handwriting
across the kitchen floor

Mother scrubbed and waxed
on her hands and knees

—Jane's mother, not mine.
Mine puffed on her cigarette,
smoke scribbling on the air
in the rooms we call our lives,

where it begins to snow
real snow outside the panes,
beyond the huge paper flakes
children fold, cut, and tape

to classroom windows,
no two flakes alike:
brief fingerprints
whorling on the glass.

Best Friend

My first best friend had pale delicate skin
and when she laughed or was embarrassed
her cheeks flared up into two hot pink spots,
for hours, like stains she couldn't rub out.
She lived walking distance from the firehouse,
so the days and nights her father was on duty,
she could see him anytime she chose,
visit the private quarters on the second floor,
above the gleaming trucks and coiled hoses
where her father lived his other life.
When I first went along with Cynthia,
I thought I'd have to shinny up the brass pole
through the hole cut in the ceiling, but we
only had to walk up stairs, to see one big
happy family of men, smoking and playing
cards around the dinner table, frying sausages
on the stove, drying socks on radiators,
their heavy black rubber coats on hooks,
flayed open, smooth as animal hides.
In the dormitory, I saw their beds made
with linens from home, shelves of personal
belongings, children's photos, lucky stones.
I petted their mascot Dalmatian while
Cynthia kissed each fireman goodbye.
Afternoons after school, we'd play quietly
in the rose garden behind her house,
so as not to disturb her father, off-duty.
Once, stumbling outside in his pajamas,

he looked perfectly ordinary, not a hero—
just like my own father, who worked regular
hours in his store. Cynthia caught me staring,
and cut in, "He's not a lazybones, really.
He's just catching up on sleep."
When a small plane crashed one foggy morning
into the radio tower a few blocks away,
and the engine sailed over town, missing
the school, landing down the street from us,
burning an apartment house to the ground,
many people died, all the passengers.
From my bedroom window I saw smoke
and, in the distance, eleven stories high,
the tower's torn and twisted scaffolding
where the plane caught in it like a fly.
A week later, as I walked Cynthia home,
she whispered that her father, the day after
the crash, sifting through the cooling rubble
in the vacant lot next door, saw something
lying in the dirt, he didn't know what,
and picked up a woman's hand severed
at the wrist, a left hand, with a diamond
engagement ring still on it. For months
the remaining fuselage lodged in the tower
like a decomposing corpse, until someone
figured out a way to bring it down.

The Sunroom

My chickenpox was itchy, like pinfeathers.
Blisters popped out on my scalp, eyelids, even my tongue,
like the plague God brought down on Egypt.
"Don't scratch!" my mother yelled.
I couldn't help but scratch.

Quarantined from my new baby sister,
I was playing in the sunroom Easter Sunday morning,
keeping track of the parade on the television—
playing in the sunroom the whole week before,
during Passover, while I was still contagious—
playing in the sunroom a month before,
the one and only time I met my grandfather,
all tanned and leathery—a cameo appearance
like a retired movie star.
He brought a crate of Florida grapefruit for the family
and a stuffed baby chick for me.

The moment I saw the chick—
its black glass eyes, its real beak
smooth as a shelled peanut
with two little slits for nostrils—
I was afraid of it.
Its insides had been scooped out
like chickens my mother koshered:
she'd stick her hand between the legs and pull out
the shiny gizzard, liver, and the gigantic ruby

of the heart, then rub the skin and the inside cavity
with Diamond Crystal Kosher Salt.

What scared me the most
was that the chick was really dead,
dead in its *actual* body, like a mummy;
its precious organs thrown away,
its body sanitized, stuffed with straw,
and covered with feathers dyed a sunny yellow.

I was sure I'd caught chickenpox
from the baby chick.
I thought I'd die.

The first Passover,
the Angel of Death had slaughtered
every Egyptian firstborn son.
Smeared blood was the sign
for the Angel to pass over.
I was a firstborn.
My body was covered with signs.

On Easter morning,
I watched them walking home from church
to eat their Easter meals —
men and boys in somber suits,
women in flowered hats,

girls wearing new spring coats on sale
at Lobels Department Store,
in lovely Easter-egg colors—soft unbleached wool
dipped into pale washes
of baby blue, mint, lavender, and pink—

pink as an Easter ham
stuck all over with cloves,
cloves like the burning scabs I scratched
as they paraded past.

The Holiday Season

The electric eye of the mezuzah
guarded our apartment over the store,
as innocent of Christmas
as heaven, where God lived,
how many stories above the world?
Was He angry when He saw
all the windows on my street—
the assimilated grocer's, druggist's,
even my father's store—
lit up like an Advent calendar?

Alone in my bedroom
the nights my parents worked late,
I'd hear voices and laughter
float up through the floor—
customers trying on dressy dresses
in the fitting rooms below.
The store was dressed up too,
with tinsel, icicles,
everything but a Christmas tree—
"Over my dead body," my mother said.

Christmas was strictly business
in my parents' store.
Fourteen shopping days to go,
my class sang carols
in front of the school assembly.
In starched white blouses

we marched up to the stage,
our mouths a chain of O's.
When we came to the refrain
"Christ the Savior is born,"

as if on cue all the Jewish kids
were silent, except me,
absent-mindedly humming along
until the word *Christ* slipped out.
It was an accident!
Gentiles believed in Christ.
We Jews believed in a God
Whose face we were forbidden to see,
Whose name we were forbidden
to say out loud, or write completely.

We had to spell it *G-d,*
the missing *o* dashing into its hole.
That afternoon after school,
I sat near an empty fitting room
folding gift boxes, carefully locking
cardboard flaps in place.
Was God going to punish me?
My father knelt in the window
like one of the Magi in a crèche,
among mannequins, dressed

and accessorized, as if they actually
had someplace to go. He dusted
off a plastic angel three feet tall.
Stored in the cellar, she lorded it
over the old broken mannequins,
naked, bald, their amputated limbs
piled in the corner like firewood.
The Sunday before holiday season
she ascended, one flight, to the store,
trailing a tail of electric cord.

After my father plugged her in,
she glowed from halo-tip to toe,
faith—a fever—warming her cheeks,
her insides lit by a tiny bulb.
I longed to smuggle her up to my room,
to have some company at night
when the store was open late.
I gazed down the darkening street,
Seventy-ninth to Boulevard East,
and out over the Hudson.

At sundown, I went upstairs.
Dinner was defrosting in the oven.
The last night of Chanukah,
eight candles, like eight crayons—
arranged from right to left,
like a line of Hebrew writing—

wobbled in the brass menorah.
My father struck the match.
Flame wavered in my hand;
I numbly sang the blessing

as if the words on my breath
could sweep away the word
I'd sung earlier that day.
Was God going to punish me?
I'd have to ask the Magic 8 Ball,
my gift on the first night of Chanukah.
For the past seven nights,
before going to sleep,
instead of saying my prayers,
I'd consulted the 8 Ball.

It could predict the future.
You asked it a yes-or-no question,
you turned it over,
and the answer slowly floated up
through the inky liquid
to the round window on top.
I held the black ball
firmly in my hands.
"Is God going to punish me?"
"CONCENTRATE AND ASK AGAIN"

I stared out my bedroom window
across the back alley
at the rabbi's house,
and watched him walk from room
to room, his windows
like frames on a strip of film.
He vanished through his kitchen door
and reappeared a moment later
a shadow, a hazy nimbus rippling
his bathroom's frosted window glass.

Swaying before his mirrored ark's
two fluorescent scrolls of light,
he performed his evening ritual—
brushing his teeth,
washing his hands, then
sinking discreetly out of sight.
For spying on the rabbi,
I'd added on another sin!
I concentrated, closed my eyes,
again I asked the question:

"Is God going to punish me?"
"REPLY HAZY TRY AGAIN"
"Is God going to punish me?"
"BETTER NOT TELL YOU NOW"

"Is God going to punish me?"
"IT IS DECIDEDLY SO"
"Is God going to punish me?"
"MY REPLY IS NO"
"8 Ball, what is your answer?"
"ASK AGAIN LATER"

I had to see what was inside.
I took a hammer to the ball
and whacked. Not a crack;
I'd barely scratched its shell.
I looked into its eye,
the dark unblinking eye,
as far as I could see inside the skull
where, floating together in ink
(so many I couldn't see them all),
were all the answers possible.

The Slap

In 1959, at Horace Mann Elementary
in North Bergen, New Jersey,
wearing white on Wednesday meant you were a virgin,
wearing red on Thursday meant you were a lesbian,
wearing green on Friday meant you were a tramp.

The gymnasium's locker room and showers
and drains moldered in the basement.
Sanitary-napkin dispensers were always empty,
and the changing rooms' private stalls'
flapping white curtains didn't quite close.
I undressed, put on my gray cotton gym suit,
and stepped out in the open with all the other girls.

The gym teacher, Miss Piano, wore a Dutch-boy haircut.
Her legs were as solid as a baby grand's.
She called us by our last names, like privates in the army,
and clapped, as each girl climbed the ropes
and disappeared into girders and beams
and caged light fixtures on the ceiling.
When my turn came,
I gripped the lowest knot and dangled down;
my legs drawn up, I looked like a dying spider.

On the bleachers, chummy as sorority sisters,
the lucky girls who had their periods
gossiped and pretended to do homework
after handing Miss Piano a nurse's note.

Where was my excuse?
After gym class, I'd undress, stuffing
my gym suit back into its mildewed bag.
But first I'd examine my underpants
for the red smear of "the curse."
The last of my friends, the last of the last.
No luck. I'd swathe myself again
in my neutral clothing.

When one morning I woke up,
two black ink blots staining my pajamas,
I dragged my mother out of bed to tell her.
We squeezed into the bathroom
as if into our clubhouse
and she was going to show me the secret handshake.

Blushing, leaking, I sat on the tub's rim,
as if poised over the mikveh, the ritual bath.
Stuffed inside my underpants,
the bulky Kotex, safety pins, and elastic sanitary belt
I'd stored in my closet for over a year.
My mother took a seat on the toilet lid.
"Ma," I shyly said, "I got my period,"
then leaned over to receive her kiss,
her blessing.

She looked as though she were going to cry.
In her blue nylon nightgown, her hairnet

a cobweb stretched over her bristling curlers,
my mother laughed, tears in her eyes,
and yelled, "Mazel tov! Now you are a woman!
Welcome to the club!"
and slapped me across the face —
for the first and last time ever —

"*This* should be the worst pain you ever know."

The House of Silver Blondes

Side by side in matching plastic capes,
my mother and I were two from a set
of Russian dolls wearing the family brand
of hair—dark, wavy brown.

A graduate of beauty school
was frosting my mother's hair today.
Only a few years older than I,
she had a honey-blonde beehive,
teased and glazed,
and a married boyfriend twice her age.

She stuffed my mother's hair
under a punctured bathing cap.
Her crochet hook pulled dark strands
one by one through the holes.
At first my mother looked bald.
And then like one of those dolls
with rooted hair you can really comb,
clumps of hair plugged into the holes
drilled in rows around their skulls.

Pulling on her rubber gloves,
the girl painted my mother's head
with bleach, a greasy paste,
then kneaded and sculpted the hair on top
into a kewpie doll's one enormous curl.

She set the timer, as if boiling an egg.
If she left it on too long, the hair
would turn auburn, red, blonde, silver,
and my grandmother's snowy white.

I paged through the latest *Seventeen*.
April's Breck Girl gazed coolly back.
With her blonde pageboy
and pink cashmere sweater,
she looked as if she belonged
in the white Cadillac double-parked out front.
She hated my babyish ponytail too!

A semester short of his degree,
the boss's son practiced on me,
bending my neck backward
onto the cold pink lip of the basin.
His every touch gave me a shock.
Even while he trimmed my hair,
I couldn't take my eyes off my mother's
bumpy rubber scalp stained with dyes
like bruises healing yellow-brown and plum.

If my mother had one life to live,
why not live it as a blonde?
Gone was her beautiful dark brown hair.
I had lost her

among the bottles of peroxide and shampoo,
rollers, bobby pins, rat-tailed combs,
and dryers' swollen silver domes.

We walked the block back to the store,
one dark and one fair,
passing the grocer, the butcher, the baker,
every window on the street a mirror.

Music Minus One

Music minus the solo melody part—with the tapes or
records providing the background music, you can play an
instrument or sing along with the band, try your hand at
Grand Opera, or even perform a concerto, surrounded by
a full symphony orchestra.
—From the Music Minus One catalogue

Sunday afternoons, my father practiced
flute in the family room.
He warmed up, playing scales,
while my mother worked the crossword puzzle
in her wing chair, like a throne.
Three o'clock and she was still
wearing her nightgown and slippers.
Our store downstairs was closed.
She was sick of looking at dresses all week.
Sunday was her day of rest.

I sprawled on the floor with my homework.
Each in our little orbit.
My father gave it all up when he married her.
Abdicated, like the Duke of Windsor.
Music was no life for a family man.
During the War, he had led the band
in the Marine Corps, in the South Pacific.
In the photo, each man poses with his instrument
except my father, holding a baton;
clarinets and saxophones leaning against their chests,
like rifles at port arms.

It was my job to start the record over.
The sheet music, stapled to the album cover,
was propped on the music stand.
The needle skated its single blade
in smaller and smaller circles on black ice.
The needle skipped. He was a little rusty.
When he lost his place, it left a hole in the music,
like silence in a conversation.

You had to imagine his life before the War.
At fifteen, on the Lower East Side, he played
weddings and bar mitzvahs;
at sixteen, he toured with the Big Bands.
You had to imagine him before
he changed his name from Joseph Sharfglass
to George Shore; you had to imagine him

handsome in his baby-blue tuxedo
when he played with Clyde McCoy's orchestra,
lighting up hotel ballrooms from New York to California
and all the road stops in between.
One enchanted evening in Connecticut,
he saw my mother.
A week later, he shipped off to the War.

You had to imagine his life before the War—
the one-night stands, the boys on the bus,
and in its wake the girls

with plucked eyebrows and strapless dresses
surrounding him like the mannequins
as he stood behind the counter
of his store, waiting for customers,
in New Jersey on the Palisades.
You had to imagine him occupying the uniform
now folded neatly in his footlocker
under the telescope pocked with rust—or bloodstains—
a souvenir from the War.
The record spun. He caught his breath.
The music raced on without him.

Meat

The year I had the affair with X,
he lived downtown on Gansevoort Street
in a sublet apartment over a warehouse.
It was considered a chic place to live.
He was wavering over whether to divorce
his wife, and I'd fly down
every other week to help him decide.
Most nights, we'd drop in for cocktails
on the Upper East Side and hobnob
with his journalist friends, then taxi
down to SoHo for an opening and eat
late dinner in restaurants whose diners
wore leather and basic black.
We'd come home at four in the morning,
just as it was starting to get light
and huge refrigerator trucks were backing up
to the loading docks and delivering
every kind of fresh and frozen meat.
Through locked window grates I could see
them carrying stiff carcasses, dripping crates
of iced chickens. We'd try to sleep
through the racket of engines and men
shouting and heavy doors being slammed.
By three in the afternoon the street would be
completely deserted, locked up tight;
at twilight they'd start their rounds again.
The street always smelled of meat.
The smell drifted past the gay bars

and parked motorcycles; it smelled
like meat all the way to the Hudson.
And though they hosed it down as best
they could, it still smelled as though
a massacre had occurred earlier that day,
day after day. We saw odd things
in the gutter—lengths of chain, torn
undershirts, a single shoe, and sometimes
even pieces of flesh—human or animal,
you couldn't tell—and blood puddling
around the cobbles and broken curbstones.
On weekends, we'd ask the taxi
to drop us off at the door
so that no one could follow and rob us.
We'd climb to our love nest
and drape a sheet over the bedroom window—
the barred window to the fire escape—
which faced across the airshaft the window
of a warehouse—empty, we assumed,
because we'd never seen lights on
behind the cracked and painted panes.
In the morning, we'd sleep late,
we'd take the sheet down and walk
around the apartment naked,
and eat breakfast in bed, and read,
and get back to our great reunions . . .
One Sunday, we felt something creepy—
a shadow, a flicker—move behind a corner

of broken glass. And we never knew
who they were, or how many,
or for how many months they had been
watching us, the spectacle we'd become.
Because that's what we were to them—
two animals in a cage fucking:
arms and backs and muscle
and flanks and sinew and gristle.

Workout

My sister is doing her exercises,
working out in my husband's study.
The rowing machine sighs deeply with every stroke,
its heavy breathing like a couple making love.

She's visiting from Iowa
where the cold weather is much worse.

When she was ten, I'd hear her
strumming her guitar through the bedroom wall.
She'd borrow my albums—my Joan Baez, my Dylan—
and sing along,
shutting me out, drawing me in;
imitating my hair, my clothes,
my generation.

I used to feel sorry for her
for being eight years younger.

She opens the door a crack, and surfaces
in earphones, and wearing pink bikini panties
and a lover's torn T-shirt.
Strapped to her hands are the weights
that weighed her suitcase down.
Her thighs are tight, her triceps shine,
her body is her trophy.

The night she arrived, we sprawled across my bed,
her cosmetic bag spilled open,
and she shadowed my eyelids violet,
demonstrating the latest tricks,
the way I used to make her up
on those nights she watched me dress for dates,
watched me slip into my miniskirt,
my sandals, my love beads.

Now she's no longer in love with me,
and eyes me pityingly,
triumphant, her expression the same as mine
when I watched my mother
examine her face in the magnifying mirror.

She's got to keep in shape.
She's a performer, it's her business
to look beautiful every night.

Sometimes, when she begins to sing,
men in the audience fall in love.

She's warming up in the shower;
the tile walls amplify her voice.
Safe, for once, under temperate rain.

Like a dress handed down
from sister to sister,
in time one body will inherit
what the other has outgrown.

The Wrong End of the Telescope

For Elizabeth Bishop

That afternoon on the Bay of Fundy,
as the car plunged in and out of the cobweb fog,
everything was in the process of erasing
or being erased.
At low tide, the tidal bore's puddle-raked mud flats
looked like a bolt of brown corduroy
running down the coast.
Later, when the sun came out, the puddles
turned into shattered mirrors, long shards,
blue sky and clouds lying in pieces on the ground,
as though the heavens had fallen down.

Stopping at a gas station for directions
and a Coke, my husband and I heard the local joke:
"You go from Upper Economy, to Middle, to Lower,
to Just Plain Broke."

The next day, on Cape Breton, pressed for time,
we wanted to drive the entire Cabot Trail
in a day. If we started at dawn
and drove clockwise around the coast,
we'd end up at dusk where we began.
The road linked town after coastal town,
each with its prim white clapboard church
starched stiff as a christening gown.
Azure woodsheds, chartreuse barns,

stilt houses shingled gray or shingled brown,
matchbox houses two stories high
painted the same pea green, ochre, or peacock blue
as the boats docked in the harbor below.
In Nova Scotia—nowhere else in the Maritimes—
fishermen paint their houses to match their boats!

It was like looking through the wrong end of a telescope,
everything scaled down, "smaller than life."
In Belle Côte, four wooden fishing boats
bobbed single-file gosling-style
in the middle of the harbor
while real full-size fishing boats
bobbed, tethered to the dock.
Were they a practical joke
or a winter evening's woodwork?
Those little boats looked too *serious* to be toys.

And that dollhouse stuck on a pole—
a whittled-down version of the gabled house
looming up behind it—
was really a mailbox!
No mail today. No one home.
Everyone seems to have vanished,
leaving their toys behind.

We counted more scarecrows than farmers
working in the fields.

No solitaries crucified on broom poles
meditating over a quarter acre of corn,
these posed in groups, in gay tableaux,
whole families of scarecrows
watching their gardens grow.
We drove past a family of scarecrow men
lovingly dressed in their Sunday best—
workshirts, overalls, and stovepipe hats.
Great-grandfather, Grandfather, Father, and Son
holding hands like a row of paper dolls,
passing on the deed to the farm
to the last son, the current one, the heir,
stretching out his hand to thin air.

A few miles up the road
a scarecrow child was dressed for winter
in dungarees, sweater, mittens, and a scarf,
standing between his scarecrow mother and father,
whose broomstick arm stuck out
in a permanent gesture of waving hello—or goodbye—
depending on the direction
you were driving to—or from.

That day, I was wearing an Indian cotton skirt
printed with huge vivid flowers.
A bee flew into the open window of the moving car
and tried to pollinate my skirt.

Given the modest scale of things,
whose idea was it to build
"the largest lobster trap in the world,"
a wooden scaffolding the size of a cathedral?
How many weathered traps had we seen
stacked by the side of the road?
A lobster trap?—it was a tourist trap!
Inside, a little gift shop
sold the usual array of junk:
lobster ashtrays, lobster key rings,
and foot-long lobster-claw combs.

Not nearly as grand, the crafts museum
masqueraded as a souvenir stand.
We arrived just before closing.
The curator had just taken out her teeth.
Tight-lipped but cheerful, she led us
through a room jammed from floor to ceiling
with antique spinning wheels.
It was like strolling through the inside of a clock.
She sat on a low stool, carding raw wool
into clouds that she proceeded to spin,
pumping her treadle like an organ pedal,
demonstrating, for at least the hundredth time that day,
one of the lost arts of the district,
kept just barely alive by her
and a few elderly lady volunteers.

Down the road lived her Micmac counterpart—
the last of her tribe who knew how
to weave baskets from sweet grass and porcupine quills.

Crayoned signs read, PLEASE DON'T TOUCH!
the swatches of Scottish tartans and coats of arms,
and the bagpipe, a droopy octopus.
Don't touch the yellowing scrimshaw,
the tiny ivory- and bone-handled tools
that tatted feverish edges on doilies and handkerchiefs
also on display. Don't touch the battered toys—
dolls, locomotives, decoys, and the love letter
whose frilly signature's a faded sepia lace.
In a separate glass case, a missionary's
English-Micmac dictionary, and a pair
of beaded moccasins with stiff enormous tongues.
Of course, you can't touch *them!*
Or the sand-encrusted gold doubloon
shipwrecked off the coast like the rising moon—
lost, all lost, and then recovered.

Missing

These children's faces printed on a milk carton—
a boy and a girl
smiling for their school photographs,
each head stuck atop a column
of vital statistics:
date of birth, height and weight, color
of eyes and hair.

On a carton of milk.
Half gallon, a quart.
Of what use is the body's
container, the mother weeping milk or tears.

No amount of crying will hold it back
once it has begun its journey
as you bend all night over the toilet,
over a fresh bowl of water.
Coins of blood spattering the tile floor
as though a murder had been committed.

Something wasn't right, they say,
you are lucky.
Too soon to glimpse the evidence
of gender, or to hear a heartbeat.

Put away the baby book, the list of names.
There are four thousand, at least, to choose from.

No need now to know their derivations,
their meanings.

Faces pass you in the supermarket
as you push the wire cart down the aisles.
The police artist flips through pages
of eyes and noses, assembling a face,
sliding the clear cellophane panels into place.

You take a quart of milk.
Face after face,
smiling obedient soldiers,
march in even rows
in the cold glass case.

Postpartum, Honolulu

Before she was born,
I was a woman who slept
through the night, who could live
with certain thoughts without collapsing...

if my husband died,
I could remarry; if I lost
my job, I could relocate,
start afresh...

I could live through "anything."
Even my daughter arriving
four weeks early,
a smile stitching my raw abdomen, hurting
as if I'd been cut in half.

When they brought her to me
for the first time, her rosiness
astonished me, she
who had been so long in the dark:

now swathed in an absurd cap and a blanket
washed, rewashed, folded precisely as origami;
a diaper fan-folded to accommodate
her tiny body, a long-sleeved undershirt
with the cuffs folded over her perfect hands,
making them stumps.

In my private room
filled with expensive gift bouquets,
the stalk-necked bird of paradise flowers,
blind under their spiky crowns of petals,
gawked at me, and the anthurium's
single heart-shaped blood-red leaf
dangled a skinny penis.

The next morning, they wheeled me to the nursery.
Behind the glass window,
the newborns were displayed, each
in its own clear plastic Isolette.
A few lay in separate cribs, under heat lamps,
and among them, mine,
born thirty days early, scrawny, naked, her skin tinged
orange with jaundice.

Under the ultraviolet lamps, her eyes taped shut,
like a person in a censored photograph,
a strip of tape slapped over her genitalia,

a prisoner, anonymous, in pain—

my daughter, one day old, without a name,
splayed naked under the lamps,
soaking up the light of this world,
a sad sunbather stretched out on Waikiki.

The Bad Mother

When we play our game, Emma
always saves the best roles for herself:
the Princess, the Mermaid, Cinderella.
Pushing her toy broom around the kitchen,
she'll put up with the dust and the suffering.
She knows she'll be rewarded in the end.

We act out one of her favorite scenes,
where the wicked stepsisters
tear Cinderella's gown to shreds—
the dress she's about to wear to the ball,
the dress sewn from scraps
of her own dear dead mother's clothes.
While I rip the invisible lace,
Emma flings herself to the floor, sobbing
until I, her Fairy Godmother, show up
and spoil her with a coach and a chauffeur,
and a ball gown tiered like a wedding cake.

I've expanded my repertoire.
I'm Snow White's vain stepmother
disguised as a pimpled crone,
a traveling saleswoman
knocking on the Seven Dwarfs' door,
selling Snow White—no, giving away for free—
my entire inventory of poison bodices, apples, combs,
to a heroine who gets instant amnesia
every time evil is about to strike.

I'm the Thirteenth Fairy
who makes Sleeping Beauty
prick her finger on a spindle
and fall into Adolescence's deep sleep
from which she'll awaken,
years later as I did, as a mother.
Over and over, I watch my daughter
fall into a faint, and die.

"Rapunzel, Rapunzel," I call from below,
eye level with the hem of the dust ruffle,
"let down your hair!"
And Emma solemnly flips her long beige braids
over the edge of the bed—wearing
a pair of my pantyhose on her head, like a wig.

The nylon feet softly brush the floor.
Now I am witch, now prince, now witch
climbing the pale ladder of Rapunzel's hair.
Pretending my fingers are scissors,
I lop off her braids, cutting off
the source of my daughter's power,
her means of escape, her route
to loving someone other than me.

Once, I played the heroine,
now look what I've become.
I am the one who orders my starving child

out of my house and into the gloomy woods,
my resourceful child, who fills her pockets
with handfuls of crumbs or stones
and wanders into a witch's candy cottage.

I am the one who sends my Vassilissa on an errand
from which it's doubtful she'll return alive
from a fate too horrible to say aloud,
a witch's hut built from her victims' bones.

I'm the one who commands the hunter to kill,
and cut out my daughter's heart
and bring it back, posthaste, as proof.
I will salt it, and eat it.
I do this as a present for my daughter.
And like the good girl I started out as,
I mind my manners.
I lick the plate clean, lick it
clean and shiny as a mirror —
Time's talking mirror — who is my daughter.

The Sound of Sense

Through the heat register I can hear
my daughter reading in the room below,
eating breakfast in her usual chair
at the kitchen table, two white pages
of her open book throwing the blinding
pan of sunlight back at her downcast face.
I hear her chirping up and down the scale
but I can't decipher a single word
as Emma learns to read. She's in first grade
and has to read a new book every day,
a weight she carries between school
and home in her backpack, in a Ziploc
baggie, with her lunch—a nibbled sandwich
squashed into an aluminum foil ball
she's crumpled hard as a chunk of pyrite.
She unzips the baggie and out falls
"The Farm," eight pages long, more pamphlet
than book. Not much happens in the plot.
A farm, a barn, a boy, a cow that moos a lot.
The words are hard, but Emma sounds them out
one at a time, the O's both long and short—
Cheerios bobbing in a lake of milk
in which her spoon trails like a drunken oar.
This morning her father, coaching her,
clears his throat, knocking his cup against *what?*
—I hear it clatter but can't make it out.
"Hurry up," he shouts, "or you'll miss the bus!"
I hear his imperative clearly enough,

but in the raised volume of her reply
the words are lost, garbled, caught in the throat
of the register's winding ducts and vents.
In an hour or so, when sunlight moves on,
a film will glaze the soured milk, like frost,
where the sodden O's float, life preservers.
Now, over muffled clinks of silverware,
clattered plates, running water, morning din,
the sound of sense resumes its little dance.
I hear my daughter turn the title page,
then silence, then a spurt of words, false start,
hesitation, a spondee of some sort,
then an iamb, then an anapest, then
a pause, another iamb—that's The End.
Then the scrape of wood on tile as Emma
pushes her chair away and clomps upstairs
to change from her pajamas into clothes.

Holocaust Museum

As we filed through the exhibits,
Charlotte and I took turns
reading captions to Andy.
Herded into a freight elevator,
we rode to the top floor,
to the beginning of the War,

descending floor by floor,
year by year, into history
growing darker, ceilings
lowering, aisles narrowing
to tunnels like the progress
of Andy's blindness.

In Warsaw, his parents owned
the Maximilian Fur Salon,
like a little Bergdorf Goodman—
doorman, and French elevator,
furs draped on Persian carpets
and blue velvet Empire chairs.

Andy was one of the lucky ones—
playing cards in the back seat
of the family Packard as they
threaded through peasant villages,
trading mink coats for gasoline—
escaping Poland the day before

the border closed. Unless Topper,
his German shepherd guide dog,
is at his side, it's hard to tell
that Andy is blind. His blue eyes
look directly at you when you speak.
Today, his gray-bearded face, grave,

as Charlotte and I described
photographs and artifacts, or read
quickly, in monotones, as if reciting
selections from a menu.
Something had to break me down—
the cattle car, crematorium door,

the confiscated valises of Jews
piled high, dramatically lit
like a department store display.
It was a small snapshot of a girl—
shot dead, lying beside her parents
on the cobbled street, her hair

as long as my eight-year-old's,
her coat, about my daughter's size.
People detoured around our little
traffic jam slowing down
the line, as Topper strained
against his leash and metal

harness. They smiled when he
flopped down, sighing, nodding off
at Andy's feet. A man
asked permission to pet him.
After all those photographs
of snarling, muzzled, killer dogs,

what a relief to see an ordinary one.
He struck up a conversation with Andy.
"I see you're blind," he said politely.
"Do you understand this
any better than I do?" And Andy
shook his head and told him no.

The Lazy Susan

After dinner, while the coffee perked
and my mother cleared the dishes,
my father would take from the shelf
the Scrabble box and the dictionary,
its black leatherette jacket as battered
as some *other* family's heirloom Bible,
its red ribbon bookmark frayed to arterial threads.

I'd sprawl on the floor a few feet away
and start my homework.
My father unfolded the game board
onto the lazy Susan's wooden turntable,
and shuffled the wood Scrabble tiles
face-down in the box.

They'd be seated in their usual places
at the dining table—husband opposite wife.
Aunt Flossie would select seven tiles from the box,
her hand skimming them like a clairvoyant's.
Then Uncle Al, to her left, would draw.
He was used to arguing cases in court,
and always winning, like Perry Mason.

Waiting his turn,
he'd bully my father about his tie,
insult my mother's coffee,
comment about my beatnik-long hair.
Then, he'd start an argument with my aunt,

adjusting his black pirate-patch
over his missing right eye, a dead ringer
for the Hathaway Shirt Man in *Life*.

I'd get up and circle the table.
Standing behind my mother's back,
I studied the letters on her rack,
her ever-changing cache of luck—
syllables, stutters, false starts,
the game's only Z or X, or Q—useless without a U
unless you were spelling IRAQ, and then
no foreign words or proper nouns allowed.

She added an S to the board, going across,
and ROSE grew into a bouquet.
Under the S, she put T-A-R,
and it spawned a STAR, going down.
My mother held in reserve her secret weapon,
a blank tile, that could substitute
for any letter in the alphabet.
They groused as she announced her score
and rotated the lazy Susan a quarter turn.

A ten-minute limit—that was their rule—
ten minutes to come up with a word.
Ten minutes. Ten minutes. Ten minutes.
Another half hour passed.
Ashtrays filled up, were emptied,

ashes drifting over the vinyl tablecloth
as, week after month after year,
the lazy Susan turned under the chandelier.
They'd play until ten or eleven, or until Al blew up
and Flossie tried to smooth things over,
my mother muttering "some things will never change."

But once, before I went off to college,
I saw them actually finish a game.

Uncle Al stared at his letters.
Aunt Flossie lit a cigarette,
and asked, "What's with Milton Marx?"
My mother said, "I saw him in the grocery.
Two days out of the hospital, he looks terrible."
My father said, "He stopped by the store.
To me, he looked okay."
My uncle said, "Milton called me on the phone.
He could barely even talk, he was so hoarse."
My aunt glanced at her rack of letters.
"Thank you thank you!" Aunt Flossie said,
and quickly put HOARSE down on the board.

With the flat of his hand,
my father swept the letters back into the box
and folded the board.
Uncle Al tallied the final scores,
the fingernails on his elegant hands

buffed and polished from his weekly manicure.
He was *ambidextrous*—
a talent he was proud of,
a word that would make a killing.

The Combination

I carried it in my wallet,
the way teenage boys used to carry
a single condom—just in case.

On my visits home, after dessert,
my father would nod to my mother,
my sister, my aunts, my uncle,
and, catching my eye, he'd give me the signal—a wink.
He'd stand up, excusing the two of us
from the coffee drinkers at the table.
We'd go downstairs,
unlock the store, deactivate the alarm,
and lock the door behind us.

I'd follow him past the dress racks
into the last fitting room in the back.
He'd draw the curtain,
unlatch the door disguised by a mirror,
and then he'd point to the family safe
hidden under a green drape,
always prefacing his apology
with, "It's only just in case,
in case something should happen.
I'm no spring chicken, let's face it."
And then he'd shrug.

I'd kneel before the squat steel box.
While he shone the flashlight on my hands,

nervous, I practiced the routine
I'd rehearsed for the last twenty years,
ever since he'd had his heart attack.
Every time the heavy door swung open,
I'd close my eyes, not wanting to look inside.

When my aunt called,
I drove north all day, checking my wallet,
checking the numbers he'd jotted down,
still legible on the torn pink slip.

Behind the faded GOING OUT OF BUSINESS sign
he placed in the window
a month before my mother died,
the empty store was a tomb,
the upstairs apartment was a tomb,
the safe had been moved to his closet.
Underneath the chorus line of laundered shirts,
the green drape shrouded the safe.

I got down on my knees.
I started with the dial turned to 0.
I turned the dial to the left two whole turns
and stopped at 79.
I turned the dial to the right one whole turn
and stopped at 35.
I turned the dial to the left
and stopped at 10.

I heard a click, turned the handle,
and pulled the heavy door.

Sliding metal drawers and shelves,
sets of keys and stacked envelopes
stuffed with green, with gold
cuff links, his gold wedding ring
and gold Jewish star, his dog tags,
expired membership cards —
musicians' union, driver's license,
smeary photocopies of birth certificates,
and the key to the safe-deposit box
(the duplicate key was locked in mine),

everything on the up-and-up,
no mistresses, no skeletons, a life
apparently as orderly
as the inside of this safe.
All those years of spinning the numbers,
rehearsing the combination —
father, mother, daughter, daughter —
until I got it right.

HAPPY FAMILY

All of them are gone
Except for me; and for me nothing is gone.
　　—Randall Jarrell, "Thinking of the Lost World"

For Howard and Emma
and Florence Abramowitz

Happy Family

In Chinatown, we order Happy Family,
the Specialty of the House.
The table set; red paper placemats
inscribed with the Chinese zodiac.
My husband's an ox; my daughter's
a dragon, hungry and cranky; I'm a pig.
The stars will tell us whether
we at this table are compatible.

The waiter vanishes into the kitchen.
Tea steeps in the metal teapot.
My husband plays with his napkin.
In the booth behind him sits a couple
necking, apparently in love.

Every Saturday night after work,
my mother ordered takeout from the Hong Kong,
the only Chinese restaurant in town.
She filled the teakettle.
By the time it boiled,
the table was set, minus knives and forks,
and my father had fetched the big brown paper bag
leaking grease: five shiny white
food cartons stacked inside.

My little sister and I unpacked the food,
unsheathed the wooden chopsticks—
Siamese twins joined at the shoulders—
which we snapped apart.

Thirteen years old, moody, brooding,
daydreaming about boys,
I sat and ate safe chop suey,
bland Cantonese shrimp,
moo goo gai pan, and egg foo yung.

My mother somber, my father drained,
too exhausted from work to talk;
clicking chopsticks
instead of words in their mouths.
My mother put hers aside
and picked at her shrimp with a fork.
She dunked a Lipton tea bag into her cup
until the hot water turned rusty,
refusing the Hong Kong's complimentary tea,
no brand she'd ever seen before.

I cleared the table,
put empty cartons back in the bag.
Glued to the bottom,
translucent with oil, the pale green bill
a maze of Chinese characters.
Between the sealed lips of each fortune cookie,
a white scrap of tongue poked out.

Tonight, the waiter brings Happy Family
steaming under a metal dome
and three small igloos of rice.
Mounded on the white oval plate, the unlikely

marriage of meat and fish, crab and chicken.
Not all Happy Families are alike.
The chef's tossed in wilted greens
and water chestnuts, silk against crunch;
he's added fresh ginger to baby corn,
carrots, bamboo shoots, scallions, celery,
broccoli, pea pods, bok choy.
My daughter impales a chunk of beef
on her chopstick and contentedly
sucks on it, like a popsicle.
Eating Happy Family, we all begin to smile.

I prod the only thing left on the plate,
a large garnish
carved in the shape of an open rose.
Is it a turnip? An Asian pear?
The edges of the delicate petals
tinged with pink dye, the flesh
white and cool as a peeled apple's.
My daughter reaches for it —

"No good to eat!" The waiter rushes over —
"Rutabaga! Not cooked! Poison!" —

and hands us a plate with the bill
buried under three fortune cookies —
our teeth already tearing
at the cellophane, our fingers prying open
our three fates.

Crazy Joey

Crazy Joey was famous,
more famous than the mayor.
Though he was as old as my father,
and tall and clean-shaven,
he wore his navy blue stocking cap
pulled way down over his ears,
dressed for winter even in June.

What was he doing
hanging around the schoolyard,
slowly pedaling his dented Schwinn
just as school was letting out?
He'd pick a kid. Boy or girl.
He'd wait until you turned the corner.
Then he'd follow you home on his bike,
an empty red milk crate strapped
to its back fender.

There were rumors
that he lived with his mother in a basement.
Rumors that he was born wrong-end first.
Rumors that his father beat him senseless.
Rumors that some boys lured him
into an alley and made him
pull down his pants and pee.
And that Crazy Joey did it, cheerfully.

When, in the seventh grade, my turn came,
I pretended to ignore him,
clutching my homework, my empty lunchbox,
never once turning my head.
Crazy Joey trailed me
past the used-car lot and the deli,
through the neighborhood
neither of us lived in,
grid of locked garages, neat shoebox lawns,
house after house after house
like televisions all tuned to the same station.

It wasn't my fault
I studied piano and ballet.
It wasn't my fault
both my parents were alive.
It wasn't my fault
I was normal, even though
I lived in an apartment over our store,
and not in a real house, either.

So I didn't take the shortcut,
or try to hide, or run crying to my father
rolling up the awning of our store,
but watched my every careful step
the day Crazy Joey chose me.

Mrs. Hitler

When my mother got into a bad mood,
brooding for days,
clamping her jaws shut, refusing to talk,
brushing past me, angry,
on her way to the kitchen,
I'd call her "Mrs. Hitler" under my breath.

I knew it was wrong, very wrong.
But when her back was turned,
I'd stick out my tongue
at Mrs. Hitler in her blue nylon nightgown
and pink foam hair rollers,
glaring at the dishes in the sink.
Sometimes I'd give her the finger,
though I knew it was wrong, very wrong.

Hitler killed Anne Frank,
whose diary was required reading
in my junior high.
My father fought Hitler during the War.
But the first time I heard Hitler's name
I was eavesdropping on my aunts
sitting around our dinner table,
whispering about "the Jewish camps."
When I burst into the room,
they switched from talking English
to Yiddish, to me pure gibberish,
my ear a funnel for their gravelly words.

Were they planning to send me back
to Camp Bell, the Jewish day camp
where, homesick, I lost my appetite
and five pounds, refusing to eat?
If they made me go next summer,
I'd go on another hunger strike.

I'd seen the *Life* magazine
hidden in my parents' bedroom—
seen the photographs of Jews,
all skin and bones,
and a picture of Hitler
and his little black push-broom mustache.

I'd seen an old newsreel on TV:
German soldiers dressed
in gray uniforms, blocks of them marching,
taking giant steps in unison
as if they were playing
Follow the Leader with their friends.

I made up a game.
While my mother cooked dinner,
I'd sit on the kitchen floor,
with a plate and a knife
and a big chunk of Muenster cheese,
and pretend I was a Jew starving to death
like the Jews I saw in *Life*.

The cheese supply allotted me—
like my father's Marine rations—
was to last exactly thirty days:
I divided my cheese into a grid
cut into thirty pieces,
I popped a tiny cube into my mouth
as if taking my daily vitamin,
and gobbled it down, then whispered,
so my mother wouldn't hear,
"I was very hungry, thank you."

A moment later, I'd gruffly reply,
"You're welcome," pretending
to be my jailer, a Nazi guard;
taking on both roles, both voices,
at once—one high, one low—
just like when I played with dolls.

Day Two dawned a minute later.
My breakfast, lunch, and dinner
melted in my mouth.
"Thank You." "You're welcome."
Day Three followed, and so on,
as I played my game, Concentration Camp.

And I fed myself
the way a mother feeds her baby.
And I ate and I ate and I ate
until all the food on my plate was gone.

The Uncanny

Saturday afternoons, they like
having me over, having
had no children together
of their own.

Late afternoon, the venetian blinds
stripe gold prison bars
on their white satin bedspread:
both of them dressed
in casual slacks and pastel golf shirts;
they played eighteen holes
earlier today.

Door ajar, I burst in,
about to ask them a question.
He sits on his side
of the bed, facing the blinds,
his back to me,
his head tilting up to hers
leaning down, as if to kiss him.

He turns and, for an instant,
I see it—see her tenderly
swabbing the empty socket
of his missing right eye, her Q-Tip
poised over the flat planes of his face
as if she's about to dot an *i*.

Losing so precious an organ
is my uncle's punishment—
a married man with two children—
for having had a long affair
with my aunt.

She has to clean it every single day,
and every single day
she changes the patch.

I didn't used to think it odd
that he lived in a house with Tess
and his kids, and also
in an apartment with my aunt.
For twenty-six years
they acted like an old married couple.
Then they made it legal.

When he wears his formal black eye patch,
Al looks like Moshe Dayan.
He couldn't get a glass eye
to replace it, one like Sammy Davis Jr.'s.
He had a little tear on his bottom lid
they couldn't sew up.

Before I was born,
driving between Flossie and Tess,
he fell asleep at the wheel.

My mother says Al is lucky
that all he lost that night
was an eye.

I catch a glimpse, just as
Flossie is about to cover it
with a folded square of gauze.
Gently, she pulls adhesive tape from a roll,
cuts the sticky white strip
into two equal lengths,
makes a big sticky X
to lay across the gaping socket
to hold the gauze in place.

She is the one who sees me first.
Surprised. When he faces me,
flashing me his one good eye,
my aunt quickly covers
his nakedness. But it's too

late, I've already seen —
where his other eye should be —
the wrinkled pocket of skin
I've always been so curious about.

The Best-Dressed Girl in School

"I could make you the best-dressed girl in school,"
my mother used to say. "But I won't.
Better that you're famous for something else,
like getting good grades
or having the best manners in your class."

My mother was famous.
She owned the best dress shop in town.
At thirteen, I could almost fit
into the size 3 petites
that hung in our store downstairs,
directly under my bedsprings.
So what if a dress hung loose on me.
Why was my mother so stingy?

The first week of school,
she drove to Little Marcie's Discount Clothes.

She beamed as she dumped the bag out
on my bed, my new fall wardrobe
piled high as a pasha's pillows:
pajamas and panties and argyle socks,
white cotton blouse with Peter Pan collar,
red tattersall jumper, dungarees,
and a blue plaid woolen skirt.
Inside every collar and waistband,
the fraying outline where the label
had been razored out.

"Don't turn up your nose," my mother said.
"What gives *you* the right to be a snob?"

Unfolding the blue plaid skirt,
she made me stand on a kitchen chair
while she chalked the endless circle of pleats.
Pins scratching my knees, she put up my hem.
The next day, I
and five other girls in Mrs. Cooper's class
wore the same Little Marcie's blue plaid skirt,
just like a parochial school uniform.

But not Stacie,
the best-dressed girl in my school,
who bought her clothes at Lord & Taylor.
I wanted what Stacie had —
her Pendleton skirt and Lanz nightgown,
her London Fog raincoat and Bass Weejun loafers —
and Stacie's mother, instead of mine.

Stacie's mother spoiled her, my mother said,
because Stacie was plain,
and her grades just average.
"She doesn't have anything else going for her,"
my mother said, "other than clothes."

Hypocrite! My mother's whole life
was about clothes!

Buying, selling, wearing, breathing, eating,
sleeping, talking clothes!
Like a musician with perfect pitch,
my mother had a natural talent for clothes.

She grew up during the Depression.
She'd had to work and work
to get to where she was today—
the owner of the best dress shop in town—
but she was sick of clothes.
Sundays, summers, Christmas Eves,
she could never take a vacation
away from clothes.

Her customers waited for her
behind dark green corduroy curtains,
in separate dressing rooms,
waited barefoot, in their bras and slips,
waited for her
to run to the racks and bring them back
the perfect garment to try on.

And I waited, too,
apprenticed to my mother's exquisite taste.
Sweeping the floor
or stacking flat hosiery boxes
behind the counter, I'd climb the folding ladder
so I could better see

my mother tease a woman's arm
into a silk sleeve of a blouse,
or help her step into a skirt,
or pull a gabardine sheath over her hips,
or drape her in challis—

I watched my mother
button them up and zip them down.
I watched her dress the entire town.
Everyone in town, but me.

Browsing in the store,
they'd pinch me on the cheek and say,
"You'll be a lucky girl when you grow up."
I wasn't so sure that it was luck.

She was the queen;
I, the heir.
It would have been a snap for her
to make me the best-dressed girl in school.
But for me she wanted better.

"Give me, give me," I'd shout in my head.
And my mother would answer,
as though she'd heard me,
"If I give you all these dresses now,
what will you want when you're fifteen?"

My Mother's Space Shoes

My mother's feet were always killing her.
All day she stood in the store
selling dresses, hobbling to the dress racks
like a Chinese woman with bound feet.

My mother's mother died of the Spanish flu
when my mother was a baby.
Raised by her grandmother,
aunts, and sisters, my mother inherited
their brown hair, their nice figures,
their hand-me-down dresses,
and their old cramped shoes.

And so her toes grew crooked and her arches fell.
I was twelve when she bought her first pair
of orthopedic space shoes. Custom made,
they cost a bundle, plus tax.
She had to go to the factory in Manhattan
and stand for fifteen minutes,
ankle-deep in a pan of wet plaster of Paris.
Six weeks later, the shoes arrived—
molded in the exact shape of her feet,
the hard, black leather already broken in,
bulging with hammertoes and bunions,
and grained like a dinosaur's skin.

She clomped to the cash register,
she clomped to fetch a customer a dress.

At noon, she clomped to the deli
and ordered a corned beef sandwich,
her rubber soles trailing black scuff marks.
It was worse than wearing
bedroom slippers in public.

Six o'clock, she clomped upstairs
and cooked us dinner, and after dinner—
my father dozing on the sofa,
my sister and I sprawled on the floor
in front of the TV—
my mother plopped down in her easy chair
with her cigarettes and newspaper,
and soaked her feet
in a dishpan of soapy water.

Why couldn't she keep her pain to herself?
I cringed, trying to ignore her
torturing herself with a pedicure—
using the fancy cuticle cutters, scissors,
clippers, and pumice stone
from the Hammacher Schlemmer catalogue.
An hour later, her feet were done,
wrinkly pink, like a newborn's.

My mother was wearing her space shoes
the day we bought my first high heels
at Schwartz & Son's, the only store in town

with an x-ray machine that showed
if your shoes fit properly
and your feet had room enough to grow.

Young Mr. Schwartz jammed my big toe
against the metal sliding ruler.
I'd grown a whole size since the fall.
He brought out the pair of ugly
"sensible shoes" my mother chose—
squat heels and square toes—
and the ones I wanted—
black patent leather pumps,
pointy-toed, dangerous.

Two inches taller, I teetered across the carpet,
toes pinching with every step,
as Old Mr. Schwartz conducted me
to the x-ray console that only he
knew how to operate.

I stepped onto the pedestal,
slid my feet into the machine:
my right foot and my left foot
were twin mummies, skeletons visible
through their wrappings,
bones glowing ghostly green and webbed
with grayish flesh, cloudy ectoplasm
of squeezed ligaments and tendons.

Like my mother, I was wearing myself inside out.
Like her, standing in that pan of plaster,
I was stuck with myself forever,
wincing, rocking backward on my heels.

Evil Eye

When my daughter was two,
watching *The Wizard of Oz* on television,
the moment the Wicked Witch appeared in a scene,
Emma would walk, as if hypnotized,
to the glowing screen and kiss
the witch's luminous green face
in the same placating way
my mother used to kiss the little silver hand,
the charm she wore on a chain around her neck.

The day Emma was born, my mother
bought a yard of narrow red satin ribbon.
She tied a bow, several bows,
and basted the loops together
until they formed a big red flower
she Scotch-taped to the head of Emma's crib
to protect her while she slept.
My mother made a duplicate
to pin onto the carriage hood.
"You can never be *too* safe," she said.

My mother used to coo in Yiddish over the crib,
"*Kineahora, kineahora,*
my granddaughter's so beautiful."
And then suddenly, as if remembering something,
something very bad, she'd go *"Pui pui pui,"*
pretending to spit three times on the baby's head.
My mother wasn't some fat *bubbe* from the shtetl.

She owned a business, drove a car.
I'd never seen her act this way before.

Sitting at her kitchen table, she lit another Kent.
"You should have given Emma an ugly name
to ward off the evil eye.
Harry Lebow, the brilliant young concert pianist
from Guttenberg?
The evil eye was jealous, so it killed him.
Mrs. Cohen, who won the lottery
and went on a spending spree?
A week later, her house caught fire.
Remember Bonnie, the doctor's daughter,
your girlfriend who died of leukemia?
Her mother wore a floor-length mink;
they had a pinball machine
in their basement rec room.
That's practically an open invitation."
My mother stubbed out her cigarette.

My hand fanned the smoke away.
"Ma, You don't really believe
in that hocus-pocus, do you?"
"Maybe not," she said, "but it wouldn't hurt."

Fairbanks Museum and Planetarium

We climb the stone staircase
of the red-brick Victorian building,
my father, my aunt, my husband carrying our baby,
escaping from the mid-July heat.
My mother is missing, dead one year.

Downstairs the museum, upstairs the planetarium;
we've waited over an hour
for the next star show to start,
rejected the brochures and guided tour,
killing time, instead, with the souvenir shop's
boxed binoculars and plastic bugs,
rocks and minerals, and packages
of stick-on, glow-in-the-dark stars.
We loiter past the Information Desk
where they've set up a card table with an exhibit
of local flora, each wildflower—
stuck in its own glass jar
propping up a smudged typewritten label:
QUEEN ANNE'S LACE, COW VETCH, wilting BLACK-EYED SUSANS—
sprinkling pollen on the tabletop
like pinches of curry power.

The high barrel-vault ceiling is made of oak,
the oak woodwork and oak balconies
shiny as the beautiful cherry-and-glass cabinets
the janitor just finished polishing,
but all the exhibits inside the cases

are falling apart, from the loons' moth-eaten
chests molting like torn pillows
to the dusty hummingbirds' ruby bibs.

We interrupt a custodian vacuuming
a polar bear with a Dustbuster.
The bear's down on the floor with us, on all fours,
pinning a seal under his mauling paw.
Shuttling the baby between us,
we shuffle past a grizzly
rearing up on his pedestal,
his shin fur scuffed and shiny
where visitors' fingers have touched.
He's in a permanent rage, his bared teeth
stained yellow-brown, as if from nicotine.

The Information Lady hands us over
to the Tour Guide.
And though it is only ourselves, and a grumpy
French-Canadian family with three wired kids
detoured from the Cabot Creamery,
she ushers us up the wooden staircase where we meet
the people from the twelve o'clock show
staggering down.

French doors open and close on the planetarium
barely bigger than a living room,
rows of wooden benches

orbiting the central console
where our bearded, ponytailed Star Guide stands
and personally greets each one of us
with a damp handshake and a "Hi."

My family sits together in one row,
obedient children on a class trip.
Present, all eyes and ears.
The sun sets, the darkness intensifies.
Our eyes adjust, our heads tilt back.
Suddenly the starless night sky, pitch black,
dark as the inside of a closet,
makes me feel like crying.
Not a splinter of light squeezes out
from under the French doors' crack.
My father and my aunt immediately doze off.
They're tired, tired of missing
his wife, her sister. Now there's nothing
but a big black hole to hold us all together,
grief's gravitational pull.

"Tim" tells us his name.
With no higher-up to direct him,
he's got his chance to play God.
He pivots at his podium, clears his throat,
and casts his flashlight baton
across his orchestra of incipient stars,
no music yet, just warming up;

only his voice and a thin beam of light
about to point out areas of interest.
My husband hands me our daughter
and I unbutton my blouse to nurse her.

Tim tells us how he used to chart the heavens
from his bedroom window in Ohio when he was a boy,
then he rehashes the *Star Wars* trilogy —
that's what first hooked him on astronomy.
He tells us about his courtship of Annie,
the home birth of his baby...
Every once in a while he remembers
to mention a star.

My father softly snores. Nights and days
are swirling all around us, moons rise and set,
seasons turn, constellations twinkle
on the cracked ceiling above our heads.
Over the planetarium's slate roof
floats our familiar sky,
two Dippers, Big and Little,
and Jupiter, Mars, and the same old moon,
big and yellow as a wheel of cheddar,
preparing to rise from behind our hill.

An hour later,
like the paired fish in Pisces
swimming in the sky, the baby and I

are still at sea, too exhausted
to crawl along the bleachers and escape.
The sun pops up, pure Keystone Kops.
My aunt startles awake, gropes for her purse.
My father snores louder.
Fading, the Milky Way shakes over his bald spot—
covered, one year ago, by a yarmulke
as he stood in the cemetery under the trees—
under the big dome of heaven
where my mother now lives.

Reprise

Rummaging through the old cassettes my father
taped off the classical radio station,
my daughter finds, among Mozart and Bach,
catalogued and labeled in his elegant hand,
Jane and Howard's Wedding: 1984.
I didn't know my father taped that, too!
Disappearing with the boom box, my daughter
shuts the master bedroom's door. An hour later,
I walk in on her gate-crashing our wedding,
sprawling on our marriage bed, ear to the speaker.
When she was younger, she used to insist
she was *there,* at our wedding, and we've told her
it's impossible, she wasn't born yet, that she
was there *in spirit.* She's not convinced—hasn't she
always been with us, even when she wasn't?

She laughs at the Wedding March while her dad
and I shakily walk down the aisle
under the rented yellow-and-white tent
filling Mike and Gail's Walnut Ave. backyard.
Eavesdropping on the prayers we repeat
after the rabbi, phrase by Hebrew phrase,
she claps when the rabbi pronounces us
husband and wife and we kiss to applause,
her future father stomps on the goblet
wrapped in the caterer's cloth napkin,
and glass shatters safely underfoot.

She rewinds the tape back to the beginning,
to what she calls the "really funny part,"
back to before our murmuring guests
sit down in the rented chairs on that
sweltering June Sunday, 96 degrees,
freesia wilting, family close to fainting,
whipped cream on the cake about to turn,
back to before we stand under the canopy,
back to before the ceremony, back to when
my father presses the Record button, clears
his throat and says into the microphone:
"Testing, testing"—a voice I last heard
years ago, a few days before he died.

Shocked, I hear my dead mother say,
"George, are you sure the tape recorder's
working?" And my father says, "I'm sure."
My mother says, "George, are you *sure*
the batteries aren't dead?" And my father
answers patiently at first, then wearily,
"Essie, I'm sure." She asks him again,
and he answers again, and here they are,
arguing in my bedroom, in the house
my mother never set foot in.
My daughter's eyes shine with laughter;
mine with tears. Although I'd give anything

to have them back, even for a moment, I clamp
my hands over my ears (just as I used to
when I was growing up) and shut them out again.

Shit Soup[*]

Other mothers have their "Everything Stew,"
"Icebox Ragout," "Kitchen-Sink Casserole."
Mine had "Shit Soup," a recipe she told me
standing in her kitchen in New Jersey.
"Find a big pot, the biggest pot you have.
Shit a quartered chicken into the pot.
If you have an old carcass lying around,
shit it in. Add three quarts of cold water
and salt, and bring to a boil. Skim off
the foam as it collects on the surface.
Slice one large or two medium onions.
Shit them in. Shit in some dill and parsley.
Dried is okay but fresh tastes better.
Cut into bite-size pieces some carrots,
a couple celery stalks. Shit them in.
Those lousy-looking zucchini squash,
withered wedges of cabbage, puckered peas.
In other words, anything in the fridge.
If you have fresh or frozen string beans,
shit them in. Shit in a few potatoes.
Peel the skin, dig out the eyes, cut off
the bad parts—and shit them in anyway,
they're filled with vitamins and minerals.
Friday's leftovers, oh, what the hell.
Shit them in, shit in twelve black peppercorns.

---

[*]In Yiddish, *shit-arein* means "to pour in."

Want to know my secret ingredient?
One ripe tomato makes the broth taste sweet.
What's under that aluminum foil?
Shit it in. A little mold won't kill you.
My recipe? I don't measure. I just shit
a little of this in, a little of that.
Your Mama's Shit Soup. Enough for a week.
With a pot of this you'll never go hungry."
Shit in "There wasn't time for me to go
to the ShopRite and buy steaks to broil
for your father's and your dinner."
Shit in "I'd like to sell the store someday
and move to Florida." Shit in the Recession,
the Second World War, the Great Depression.
Shit in "There's no rest for the weary."
Shit in her bunions, her itchy skin.
Shit in "Rich or poor, it's nice to have money."
Shit in "Marriage isn't made in heaven."
Shit in the Republicans. Shit in her tumor.
Shit in where it spread to her liver
"like grains of rice," the doctor said.
Shit in her daughters at the cemetery
crying over the hole when they lowered
her in. Shit in one last handful of dirt.
Cover the pot and reduce heat to low.
Simmer on the lowest possible flame
for two hours, or until vegetables
are fork tender, meat falls off the bone.

My Mother's Mirror

After her funeral, I swiped it,
swaddled it, and spirited it home.
I'd have preferred a plain unfussy one,
not this pewter cupid caryatid
bracing up a shining circle
flipping, two-faced, like a coin—
a regular mirror on one side,
a magnifying mirror on the other.

It was my mother's best friend,
worst enemy. As a girl, I watched her
stare into it for hours, examining
her wrinkles, tweezing her eyebrows.
Sometimes I'd walk in on her
inspecting her face pore by pore,
brow to chin. Once a week,

she'd smear her face with a white clay
beauty mask that hardened like porcelain,
broken only by the glittering peepholes
of her dark brown eyes.
She appraised her face
as if she were considering
a damaged antique vase, and weighing
the severity of its cracks.

Her jaw sagged, her chin doubled,
little bags puffed out

under her eyes.
Her right eye, then her left,
clouded over with cataracts.
The mirror never changed.

The day after her funeral, my sister
and I sat and divided up her things.
I got the diamond engagement ring,
the longer string of pearls.
I was the older daughter, the firstborn.
I felt I had the right.

Now, at fifty,
I stare into her mirror
glazed with our common face,
the face I'll pass down to my daughter,
who watches from behind me
with the same puzzled look I had
when I watched my mother,
out of the corner of her eye,
watching me.

But when I swivel the mirror
to its other side,
the face tilting up at me slides away
and returns twice its size,
with swollen nose, bulging eyes, unstable
flesh stretching like the taffy body

in the funhouse mirror
at Palisades Amusement Park,
where I used to go and gaze
at the girl I was.

I look away. What did I think?
That I'd stay fourteen forever?
"By the time you're fifty,"
my mother used to say,
"you get the face you deserve."

Happiness

Joyce opens her antique silk-covered box
and we shuffle twelve dozen ebony tiles
face-down on my kitchen table.
She calls this the "Twittering of the Sparrows."
She's teaching my daughter, Emma, and me
how to play mah-jongg, the game
all the Jewish mothers played, except mine.

It's way past Emma's bedtime,
the harvest moon having risen hours ago
round and full as the one-dot
on its tile of worn ebony.
After we've stacked the tiles
and built a square Great Wall of China,
Joyce hands Emma a tiny box carved from bone,
which holds two tiny ivory dice,
small as her baby teeth I tucked away
in an envelope in my keepsake drawer.

This is weird. My generation of women
wouldn't be caught dead playing mah-jongg,
the game all the Jewish mothers played
summers at Applebaum's Bungalow Colony,
red fingernails clicking against the tiles.

Joyce's friend Susan taught her mah-jongg;
and like a big sister, Joyce wanted to teach me;

her favorite Bakelite bracelets
clunking noisily around her wrist.
Beginners, we are not yet ready
to gamble with real money.
We lay our tiles face-up on the table,
exposing our hands, so everyone can see.

At Applebaum's my mother would watch
the other mothers playing mah-jongg—
but she wouldn't sit down and join them.
Even when she took the summer off,
my mother was not about playing.

I roll the highest score on the dice,
so I am the East Wind, the dealer.
But I'm sitting at the foot of the table,
where the south, on a map, would be.
It's not the normal geography.
The South Wind sits to the left of me
clunking her bracelets,
and Emma's the North Wind, on my right.
Joyce tells us a little trick to remember
the clockwise order of play—
"Eat Soy With Noodles,"
(East, South, West, North)—
and to remind us who'll be the East Wind next.

Oh how I love the sound of the tiles
clicking together, the sound our nails make
clicking against the tiles,
the sound the ebony tiles make
scraping the oak table, the sound the dice make
bouncing softly on the wood,
the sound my mouth makes calling out
"Eight crack" and "Five bamboo" as I discard them,
the sounds the ivory counting sticks make
when we add up our scores,
and the names of the hands we have scored,
syllables of pure pleasure:

combinations of Pungs, Chows, Kongs,
and pillows, pairs of East Winds or Red Dragons,
making a Dragon's Tail, Windfall, LillyPilly,
Seven Brothers, Three Sisters, Heavenly Twins,
making a Green Jade, Royal Ruby, White Opal,
Red Lantern, and Gates of Heaven...

Why did my mother deny herself?
Once when I asked her, she confessed
that she never really enjoyed business.
I think that my mother
didn't much like mothering, either.
It scared her, too, the closeness of every day.
It was easier to fold my clothes

than to touch me. Even as she was dying,
she shut me out, preferring to be alone.
Now, she's like the West Wind in the empty chair
opposite me, the absent one we skip over
because we are playing with only three.

Emma shouts, "Mah-jongg!"—she's won her first game.
Joyce is so thrilled, she forgets
we're not playing for money.
Rummaging in her purse, she pulls out
a dollar bill and crushes it into Emma's hand.

We reshuffle the tiles. Twitter the sparrows—
all peacocks, dragons, flowers, seasons
hide under their black blankets of night.
Reflecting us, the dark window blurs our hands
then brightens into all the other hands I saw
around card tables set up under shade trees
during those long hot afternoons
in Rockland Lake, New York.
Babies napping, husbands away at work,
all the other mothers playing—
happy, sipping their iced drinks,
happy, smoking their cigarettes.

A YES-OR-NO ANSWER

I'll forgive and I'll forget, but I'll remember.
—Yiddish proverb

For Emma

A Yes-or-No Answer

Have you read *The Story of O?*
Will Buffalo sink under all that snow?
Do you double-dip your Oreo?
Please answer the question yes or no.

The surgery—was it touch-and-go?
Does a corpse's hair continue to grow?
Remember when we were simpatico?
Answer my question: yes or no.

Do you want another cup of joe?
If I touch you, is it apropos?
Are you certain that you're hetero?
Is your answer yes or no?

Did you lie to me, like Pinocchio?
Was forbidden fruit the cause of woe?
Did you ever sleep with that so-and-so?
Just answer the question: yes or no.

Did you nail her under the mistletoe?
Will you spare me the details, blow by blow?
Did she sing sweeter than a vireo?
I need an answer. Yes or no?

Are we still a dog-and-pony show?
Shall we change partners and do-si-do?

Are you planning on the old heave-ho?
Check an answer: Yes ❑ No ❑

Was something blue in my trousseau?
Do you take this man, this woman? Oh,
but that was very long ago.
Did we say yes? Did we say no?

For better or for worse? Ergo,
shall we play it over, in slow mo?
Do you love me? Do you know?
Maybe yes. Maybe no.

The Streak

Because she wanted it so much, because
she'd campaigned all spring and half the summer,
because she was twelve and was old enough,
because she would be responsible and pay for it herself,
because it was her mantra, breakfast, lunch, and dinner,
because she would do it even if we said no—

her father and I argued until we finally said
okay, just a little one in the front
and don't ask for any more, and, also,
no double pierces in the future, is that a deal?

She couldn't wait, we drove straight to town,
not to our regular beauty parlor, but the freaky one—
half halfway house, half community center—
where they showed her the sample card of swatches,
each silky hank a flame-tipped paintbrush dipped in dye.

I said no to Deadly Nightshade. No to Purple Haze.
No to Atomic Turquoise. To Green Envy. To Electric Lava
that glows neon orange under black light.
No to Fuchsia Shock. To Black-and-Blue.
To Pomegranate Punk. I vetoed Virgin Snow.
And so she pulled a five out of her wallet, plus the tax,
and chose the bottle of dye she carried carefully
all the car ride home, like a little glass vial
of blood drawn warm from her arm.

Oh she was hurrying me! Darting up the stairs,
double-locking the bathroom door,
opening it an hour later, sidling up to me, saying, "Well?"
For a second, I thought that she'd somehow
gashed her scalp. But it was only her streak, Vampire Red.

Later, brushing my teeth, I saw her mess—
the splotches where dye splashed
and stained the porcelain, and in the waste bin,
Kleenex wadded up like bloodied sanitary napkins.
I saw my girl—Persephone carried off to Hell,
who left behind a mash of petals on the trampled soil.

My Mother's Chair

Coming home late, I'd let myself in
with my key, tiptoe up the stairs,
and there she was, in the family room,
one lamp burning, reading her newspaper
in her velvet-and-chrome swivel chair

as though it were perfectly natural
to be wide awake at 2 A.M.,
feet propped on the matching
ottoman, her orthopedic shoes
underneath, two empty turtle shells.

Like a mummy equipped for the afterlife,
she'd have her ashtray and Kents handy,
her magnifying mirror,
and tweezers and eyeglass case,
her crossword puzzle dictionary.

Glancing up and down, she never
appeared to be frisking me, even when,
just seconds before, coming home
from a date, at the front door,
I'd stuck my tongue into a boy's mouth.

I'd sit on the sofa and bum her cigarettes,
and as the room filled up with smoke,
melding our opposite temperaments,

we'd talk into the night, like diplomats
agreeing to a kind of peace.

I'd feign indifference—so did she—
about what I was doing out so late.
When I became a mother myself,
my mother was still the sentry at the gate,
waiting up, guarding the bedrooms.

After her funeral, her chair sat empty.
My father, sister, husband, and I
couldn't bring ourselves to occupy it.
Only my daughter climbed up its base
and spun herself round and round.

In the two years my father lived alone
in the apartment over their store,
I wonder, did he ever once
sit down on that throne, hub
around which our family had revolved?

After my father died, the night
before I left the place for good,
the building sold, the papers signed,
before the moving vans drove away,
dividing the cartons and the furniture

between my sister's house and mine,
a thousand miles apart,
I sat on the sofa—my usual spot—
and stared at the blank TV, the empty chair;
then I rose, and walked across the room,

and sank into her ragged cushions,
put my feet up on her ottoman,
rested my elbows on the scuffed armrests,
stroked the brown velvet like fur.
The headrest still smelled like her!

Swiveling the chair to face the sofa,
I looked at things from her point of view:
What do you need it for?
So I left it behind, along with the blinds,
the meat grinder, the pressure cooker.

The Closet

Wearing her baby-blue nylon nightgown,
not the muslin shroud we buried her in,
my mother stands before my closet, puzzled.
Why are *her* dresses mingling with mine?

For once, my mother doesn't talk.
She bears no message from Jewish heaven
where the dead have nothing to do all day
but sit around and advise the living.
More like the Ten Commandments:
Never wear white in winter or velvet in summer.
Buy life insurance. File a will.

Does she want me to choose an outfit for her?
This is a first. *She* was always the expert on clothes.
Perhaps when you die, the first thing to go
is your fashion sense, because in Paradise
everyone's dressed the same.

I remember how, in her store, she'd
run her eyes over the racks of merchandise
and know exactly which dress
her customers should wear
to their fundraisers, cocktail parties, christenings.

But where's she going that's so important?
Since she's lost all that weight
her dresses just hang off her,

so she might as well be naked.
Yet her eyes seem to be begging me
to help her, help her slip back again
into the shackles of clothes.

Possession

Nesting in my nest, she slept on my side
of the double bed, stacked the books —*my* books —
she was reading on my nightstand.
In the closet, her dresses pressed
against my husband's pants.
These I boxed up for her mother,
with the baby's toys.
I tossed her blue toothbrush
and her tortoiseshell comb in the trash.

Police took away a rug. My two best knives.

But the kitchen still smells of her spices —
her cinnamon, curry, cloves.
The house an aromatic maze
of incense and sachet.
Almost every day now something of hers
turns up. The way La Brea tar pits
keep disgorging ancient bones, squeezing them
through the oily black muscles of earth
to the surface.

A yoga mat.
I don't need it. I already have my own.
Prayer beads. A strapless bra.
A gold ring. It's pretty.
It fits my pinkie.

I wash my face with her special soap,
a cool oval of white clay,
one thick black hair still glued to it.
And is it wrong to brew her herbal teas, try her
aromatherapies, her homeopathic cures,
the Rescue Remedy she'd told me
really worked? The amber bottle's full.
Why waste it? So I deposit
four bitter drops on my own tongue.

Trouble Dolls

Guatemalan Indians tell of this old custom. When you have troubles, remove one doll from the box for each problem. Before you go to sleep, tell the doll your trouble. While you are sleeping, the doll will try to solve it. Since there are only six dolls in a box, you are allowed only six troubles a day.

Every morning, I unbend
their wire limbs and lay them
back in their tiny box where
they sleep all day like vampires.

Their lidless eyes cannot close—
the pupils dots of black paint,
bull's-eyes ringed
with insomnia's dark circles.

Scalps sprinkled with black salt.
Arms opened wide,
as if expecting to be hugged
or crucified.

What were their troubles
before they came to me—
these brothers, husbands, wives,
this neighbor's son-in-law,

born in the old country
where churches collapsed

on their babies, and police
dragged off the baker,

soldiers raped the sister,
and a brother came home
with his arms twisted, and
the father with no arms at all?

Single file, they descend
the mineshaft of my unconscious,
with only a pickax and hardhat
beam to light their path.

Yet I worry that one night,
opening their box, I'll find
five dolls left, and the next night
four, subtracting a doll a day—

until, like the Disappeared,
they'll all vanish without a trace,
leaving me to worry all alone
in bed with their empty coffin.

The Blue Address Book

Like the other useless
things I can't bear
to get rid of—her
nylon nightgowns,

his gold-plated
cufflinks, his wooden
shoetrees, in a size
no one I know can use—

I'm stuck with their blue
pleather address book,
its twenty-six chapters
printed in ballpoint pen,

X'd out, penciled in,
and after she passed away,
amended in his hand,
recording, as in a family

Bible, those generations
born, married, and since
relocated to their graves:
Abramowitz to *Zimmerman.*

Great-uncles, aunts,
cousins once removed,

whose cheeks I kissed,
whose food I ate,

are in this book still
alive, immortal, each
name accompanied
by a face:

Fogel (Rose and Murray),
474 13th St., Brooklyn,
moved to a condo
in Boca Raton; *Stein*

(Minnie, sister of Rose),
left her Jerome Ave.
walk-up for the Yonkers
Jewish Nursing Home.

The baby-blue cover
has a patina of grease,
the pages steeped
in cigarette smoke

from years spent in my
parents' junk drawer.
Though scattered
in different graveyards,

here they're all
accounted for.
Their souls disperse,
dust motes in the air

that I inhale.

Dummy

He lolled on my twin bed waiting for me
to get home from Girl Scouts or ballet,
but I couldn't really play with him
the way I'd played with my other dolls—
buttoning their dresses, buckling their shoes,
brushing and braiding their long, rooted curls.
He had the one crummy green gabardine suit.
His ketchup-colored hair was painted on.
And while my baby dolls could drink
from a bottle, cry real tears, blow bubbles,
and pee when I squeezed their tummies,
my dummy didn't have the plumbing.

The water bottles I'd jam in his mouth
scuffed his lipstick, mildewed his stuffing.
Prying his smile apart, I'd run my finger
along the seven milk teeth lining his jaw.
But look inside his head. Completely empty!
No tongue, no tonsils, no brain.
No wonder he had to wear his own name
on a label sewn above his jacket pocket
to remind himself that he was Jerry Mahoney
and his straight man an eleven-year-old girl
who jerked the dirty pull string at the back
of his neck, making his jaw drop open,

his chin clack like the Nutcracker's.
That lazy good-for-nothing! I had to put

words in his mouth. His legs hung limp,
his arms flopped at his sides. He couldn't
wink or blink or quit staring to the left;
brown eyes painted open, perpetually
surprised at what he'd blurt out next:
"Grandma Fanny has a big fat fanny!
Uncle Fred should lose that lousy toupee!
Aunt Shirley dresses like a goddamn tramp!
That son of hers, Moe, a moron!"—
what *they* said behind each other's backs!

He did a slow one-eighty of my bedroom.
"How the hell did I wind up in this joint?"—
that low, unnatural voice straining through
my own locked teeth. "Good evening, ladies,"
he leered at the dolls propped on the shelf,
cocking his head to see their underpants.
How old was that wiseacre supposed to be?—
thirteen? thirty? my father's age?—the little
man sitting on my lap, telling dirty jokes
until his pull string snapped, a fraying ganglion
lost inside his neck beyond the tweezers' reach,
a string of words unraveling down his throat.

After that, we practiced our act in the dark
where I couldn't see his imperfections.
We'd talk, long after the others were asleep:
I'd move my lips, lower my voice an octave;

and it almost sounded like a conversation
between a husband and a wife.
I tweaked his bow tie, smoothed his satin dickie,
rapped on his skull. *Knock, knock.* "Who's there?"
just like in the old days when he was in mint
condition, a smart aleck; before he became
slack-jawed, dumb—a dummy forever—and I
grew up, went solo, learned to speak for myself.

Shopping Urban

Flip-flopped, noosed in puka beads, my daughter
breezes through the store from headband to toe ring,
shooing me away from the bongs,
lace thongs, and studded dog collars.
And I don't want to see her in that black muscle tee
with SLUT stamped in gold glitter
shrink-wrapped over her breasts,
or those brown and chartreuse retro-plaid
hip-huggers ripped at the crotch.

There's not a shopper here a day over twenty
except me and another mother
parked in chairs at the dressing room entrance
beyond which we are forbidden to go.
We're human clothes racks.
Our daughters have trained us
to tamp down the least flicker of enthusiasm
for the nice dress with room to grow into,
an item they regard with sullen, nauseated,
eyeball-rolling disdain.

Waiting in the line for a dressing room,
my daughter checks her cleavage.
Her bellybutton's a Cyclops eye
peeking at other girls' armloads of clothes.
What if she's missed something—
that faux leopard hoodie? those coffee-wash flares?

Sinking under her stash of blouses,
she's a Shiva of tangled sleeves.

And where did she dig up that new tie-dyed
tank top I threw away in '69,
and the purple wash 'n' wear psychedelic dress
I washed and wore
and lost on my Grand Tour of Europe,
and my retired hippie Peace necklace
now recycled, revived, re-hip?

I thought they were gone—
like the tutus and tiaras and wands
when she morphed from ballerina
to fairy princess to mermaid to tomboy,
refusing to wear dresses ever again.
Gone, those pastel party dresses,
the sleeves, puffed water wings buoying her up
as she swam into waters over her head.

My Mother's Foot

Putting on my socks, I noticed,
on my right foot, an ugly bunion and hammertoes.
How did my mother's foot
become part of me? I thought I'd buried it
years ago with the rest of her body,
next to my father in Cedar Park Cemetery.
How did it ever track me down,
knowing exactly which brick house
on the street was mine,
never having set foot in it alive?

During dinner, my husband was polite.
My daughter excused herself to do homework.
When it got too late to phone a hotel,
I invited the foot to spend the night.
I made up the studio couch, tucked the foot in,
tiptoed back to my bedroom.
A minute later came a knock at my door.
I'm lonesome, the foot sobbed.
I'm not used to sleeping alone. Whereupon
it hopped into bed between my husband and me.

Next morning, the foot woke up
on the wrong side of the bed.
Its instep hurt. Its big toe was out of joint.
So I kissed it, gave it a pedicure,
polished its five wiggling toenails Shanghai Red.
Life's really good here, the foot said.

So much better than where I've just come from.
Mind if I use your phone?
I've got a pal who has one foot in the grave.

That night, my mother's left foot joined us.
Now they're both giving me advice:
Your bathroom is filthy.
That dress makes you look fat.

Along with her pearls, her diamond ring,
and her gold earrings, I've got
my mother's knees, her varicose veins,
flabby belly, sagging breasts —

In time I'll inherit whatever's left of her body.

Keys

What do I do with the Post-it notes
she stuck on the fridge?
Do I delete her e-mail asking
was it okay
if her little boy played
with my daughter's old keychains
stored in the shoebox under her bed?

Yes, of course. Be my guest.
While you're housesitting,
Mi casa es su casa, I said.
Then I showed her
how to lock the front door
and handed her the keys.

Such a nice little boy, said our neighbor.
Such an attentive mother.
Tony, the locksmith down the street,
would reach inside a grimy jar,
as if fishing for a candy,
and hand the boy another key or two—

a bent key, a worn-down key,
a key with broken teeth,
old mailbox keys, luggage keys, and sometimes
as a special treat he'd let the boy
choose a shiny blank from the rotating display

and cut him a brand-new key
to add to his collection.

The morning she locked the doors
and turned on the alarm,
and stabbed her son and slit her wrists
and lay down on my dining room floor
to die, she left a message
on my best friend's voice mail:
Let yourself in.
Bring your spare key...

Now, it's as if my house
keeps playing tricks on me.
I open my lingerie drawer and find a key.
Whose is it?
Which lock does it belong to?

I find a key under the coffee table.
A key wedged between sofa cushions.
A key with a tag to a '71 Chevy.
Cleaning under my daughter's bed,
I find rings of keys, lots more keys,
none of which fits any lock in my house.

Trick Candles

After Cavafy

Flickering above the pink rosettes
and your name iced in ivory buttercream,
a bouquet burns on top of your cake,
fifty blossoms of flame.
One candle equals a year of your life,
plus one more to wish on.
Hurry, make a wish, blow them out!
They're out. Now cut the cake.

But wait—a guttered wick sputters and sparks
as if it suddenly has a mind of its own—
now another is lighting up,
and one by one, the dead reawaken.

Rekindled years return like little waves of nausea.
Here's 1947, the year you were born.
And 1954, when your mother had your sister.
Now 1993 joins the crowd—that miserable December
you buried your father.
Blow it out, you'll forget again.

But the dead don't stay dead.

Mother and Father, conspiring behind the door,
dimmed the chandelier in the dining room
where you sat, a child at the head of the table,

in your pinafore, your paper party hat,
feigning surprise as the solemn
procession sang "Happy Birthday,"
your future lighting up before you.

There were fewer candles then.
You could blow all of them out at once.
But now, dozens of candles —
you can't draw a breath
deep enough to extinguish them all.

Gasping, you stand like a fool
before the growing years of your past
and the dwindling years of your future —
choking on smoke, putting out wildfires
while fresh ones spring up around you.

My Father's Visits

After she died, we told him, repeatedly,
to think of our house
as his. By seven, he was fully dressed
in slacks and a laundered shirt.
He made his own breakfast,
carried his coffee cup to the sink, and washed it.
He never opened the refrigerator
without asking our permission first.
All day he sat on the sofa, reading.
He reeled off his lists of medicines, blood counts,
tagging along to the grocery, the post office,
the kindergarten at three-fifteen,
grateful for any excuse to leave the house.

Suppose my father comes back again.
Suppose he comes back, not briefly—
as when the dead show up in dreams—
but on an open return ticket.
I'm sure I'll feel shy, tongue-tied, and formal,
the way I did when I ran into my old lover
years after we'd broken up.

I won't ply him with questions
about life on the other side.
I'll put clean sheets on the sofa bed.
All the jokes I've saved up to tell him—
I'll knock myself out to make him laugh.

Every morning I'll squeeze fresh orange juice,
fry two eggs over easy, just the way he likes them,
even when he says to please ignore him,
pretend he isn't here.

Unforgettable

I'm here to kidnap my beloved aunt
from her apartment in Fort Lee, N.J.,
Flossie, my mother's older sister,
born the year the *Titanic* sank.

But before she'll let me kidnap her,
she hijacks me, steering her spiffy
high-tech walker across the street
into rush-hour traffic to the bank.

Breathless, I plead for her to stop.
Bypassing the flashing ATM,
waving her cane, she makes a scene,
repeating yesterday's, before I came,

when she demanded that the teller
withdraw $5,000 in fives and tens,
and make it snappy, from her account.
The bank called the cops, the cops

called her doctor, her doctor
called me to please come ASAP,
extract her from her apartment house
and move her into assisted living.

She calls her walker her "wagon."
She calls me by my mother's name.

Now that both my parents are gone,
I am the responsible party.

I'm responsible and it's no party.
After accusing her optometrist
of losing her bifocals, my aunt
pocketed his ballpoint pen,

the same pen she uses to sign for
the five grand in soft bundled bills
we stuff into tote bags like robbers.
She's the brains. I'm her accomplice.

They can't arrest us. There's no law
against withdrawing money that is
rightfully yours. Back from the bank,
she's too busy dumping her loot

into a drawer to catch me slipping
her car keys into my purse.
She insists on cooking us dinner.
My mouth waters for her brisket,

the only dish she's famous for.
Instead, she fills a pot with milk,
stirs in a spoon of instant oatmeal,
turns on the gas, opens the fridge,

and stares inside as if she's opened a book
and lost her place. Is she hungry?
Where's her appetite? Come to think of it,
where's her full-length sable coat?

Not in the closet where I saw it last.
Did she throw it down the incinerator
chute along with the garbage bags
she ghost-walks past the corridor's

numbered doors twenty times a day?
Is that fur warming a neighbor's back?
Lost, her husband's star-sapphire ring,
her strand of graduated cultured pearls,

her Chanel handbag, not a knockoff.
Lost, her lovely, sophisticated things.
Where did they go? Misplaced? Stolen?
She won't let strangers inside her door,

no social worker, not even the super.
She points to snapshots of my daughter
among the rogue's gallery on her desk:
"She's very pretty, what's her name?"

She says it again two minutes later.
And says it again five times more.

Though I'm afraid to leave her alone,
I lock the bathroom against her.

I don't want Auntie to see me cry.
I sit down on the closed toilet lid,
turn on the faucet, flush the toilet,
in case she's listening at the door.

But she isn't. She's where I left her,
humming happily, perfectly in tune,
"Unforgettable."
Unforgettable, that's what you are.

Dream City

> One night, Chen Chu dreamt that he was a butterfly. In
> his dream, he had never been anything but a butterfly.
> When he woke up he didn't know if he was Chen Chu
> dreaming that he was a butterfly or a butterfly dreaming
> that he was Chen Chu.
> —Zen koan

I was sleeping in a round room made of stone.
A voice called out, "This is your room. This is your bed."
For months thereafter, I crossed a river
on thoroughfares to a city that seemed familiar.
Most nights I'd return there.
Its turn-of-the-century architecture,
wrought-iron and stone apartment houses,
looked like the buildings on Park Avenue, and Fifth.
Sometimes I dreamed hybrids of buildings
over and over: a library–hotel, a train station–school;
and a department store with a rickety elevator that took me
to the fourth floor, where the dresses were.

In one dream, I caught myself telling someone,
"These are the clothes I wear in my dreams,"
as I opened a closet. Inside were
shoes, jumpers, coats, a green hat with a feather—
my taste, my size, they even *smelled* like me.

And, once, I brought someone along with me from *here*.
Here, where I am when I'm wide awake.
I said, "This is the place I always dream about."

As I fall asleep, my dream picks up in the place
where it left off the night before—
the street, the house, the room.
The next day, I might catch a glimpse of it
superimposed on what I'm *really* seeing—
a shard of light bleeding onto a negative.

In time, I began to see my city,
the basso continuo playing behind the melody
of my everyday life, as a kind of everyday life, too:
its industry, the bustle of its people,
its traffic, its history, its parallel *ongoingness*—

But not long ago, I was traveling
along the Jersey side of the Hudson
where I grew up. I hadn't been back in years:
the woods were gone—
the collapsing docks and broken pilings
replaced with high-rent condos, supermarkets, malls,
anthills in the shadow of the Palisades.

The bridge and tunnel traffic was awful.
Instead of taking a bus, I crossed
to Manhattan by commuter ferry.
In the middle of the river, I looked up
at the skyline, the buildings
bronzed by late-afternoon light—

my dream city's light —
the city I'd dreamed since I was twelve —

but I wasn't dreaming.
My husband and daughter were sitting on the bench
on either side of me.
Rows of strangers, too.
Some gazed at the skyline, as I did.
Others read their newspapers, or dozed.

Body and Soul

> The soul remains attached to the physical body after death
> for the first seven days, when it flits from its home to the
> cemetery and back. This explains why the initial mourning
> period is one week. For twelve months after death the soul
> ascends and descends, until the body disintegrates and the
> soul is freed.
> —*Dictionary of Jewish Lore and Legend*

Which must be the reason why,
lying awake in my mother's bed
the night after her funeral, I caught her
rummaging in the underwear drawer.

What a relief to know
the dead are *expected* to come back—
so seeing them up and about so soon
is no big deal.

If you die, say, in July,
I'd like to think that in the next few weeks,
your soul clings like the bar code
to the book of your body.
Little by little, the label
starts to peel, curling and lifting
until the sticky underside loses its grip.

By Labor Day, your body
can walk your soul on a leash,
yanking it back when it lifts a hind leg
over the perfect green of a neighbor's lawn.

Around Halloween, the soul begins to rise.

Thanksgiving,
it's a kind of beach ball clearing the net.
On New Year's Day, it flips on the trampoline
of the body, bouncing higher and higher
until it shoots through the roof.

As Pesach approaches,
the soul—tied by the ankles—
bungee-jumps from the body,
which, meanwhile, has been attending to
its own messy business in the ground.

How else to explain why
Judah ha-Nasi would suddenly appear
to his family on Friday nights,
dressed in his Shabbat finery,
recite Kiddush over the wine, and vanish.

Or why my mother, just last week,
stood behind me by the stove,
telling me my kugel needs more salt.

A retired dentist from Great Neck
swears he's photographed a soul leaving its body.
And a deposed countess from Romania

topped *that,*
claiming she's measured its weight in ounces.

On my mother's Yahrzeit,
when our family gathers at the cemetery
to unveil her headstone,
and we're crying, why be sad?
Think of it as a bon voyage party—
a soul at last at liberty
to make its own plans.

God's Breath

If God can be said to breathe the soul
into each living thing, as he did into Adam,
then the magician we hired
for our daughter's birthday party was like God.

Before performing the rabbit-in-the-hat trick,
before pulling shiny nickels
from Emma's ears,
he got a long skinny green balloon
and stretched it like saltwater taffy,
then put his lips to its lip and blew.

And it grew and grew,
luminous and green, it grew
in its nakedness, and when it was a yard long
the magician knotted it,
and with a few deft flicks twisted it
into a dachshund—buoyant, electric, tied to a leash
of fuchsia ribbon—that bounced
along the floor, bumping after our daughter
on their walks around the house.

Weeks later, cleaning under her bed,
I coaxed it out with a broom—
a collapsed lung furred with dust.
As long as it still had some life in it,
I couldn't throw it away.

So I popped it with a pin.
And God's breath, a little puff
from elsewhere, brushed my cheek.

On the Way Back from Goodwill

After Uncle Al's final coronary,
Aunt Flossie gave my dad
Al's unworn, tasseled, white
patent-leather penny loafers,

the Florsheim labels still stuck
like chewing gum to the heels.
Shoes my elegant father
was too polite to refuse.

So his brother-in-law's shoes
cured in a closet for twenty years,
soles stiff as planks, until
I boxed them up

with my father's things
and shipped them home,
where side by side
in the dark crawl space

under my roof they idled
for another twenty, enduring
long ice-hatcheting winters
Uncle Al would have hated.

Now the last of him
is gone, with his temper

tantrums, and his bad taste,
and his black eye-patch

that covered the empty
socket of his right eye,
lost in a car crash. Gone,
the thick wad of fifties

he carried in his pocket
to intimidate and impress.
No cheapskate, I slip
a dime into the stubborn

slot on his loafers meant
for pennies, the way
you'd close a dead man's
staring eyes with a coin

so he won't take you
along with him.
Haven't I already
done my time?

Fugue

It was not our story. It was hers.
That's how friends told us to think of it.
It was not our story, it was hers.
In what book does it say that you're
supposed to live until you're eighty?
Our house was hers for the summer.
Our forks and spoons and knives.
She seemed happy waving goodbye.
We said, *So long, take care, enjoy.*
It was not our problem, it was hers.
Her clothes hung in our closets.
Her little boy slept in our daughter's bed
and played with our daughter's old toys.
It was not our sadness. It was hers.
Her sadness had nothing to do with us.
She borrowed books from the library.
Scrubbed the bathtub. Baked a pie.
We were just going about our business.
We were hundreds of miles away.
It was not our madness, it was hers.
She finished the book. Sealed
the letter in the envelope, telling why.
We replaced the bloody floorboards
where their two dead bodies lay.
We stained the new boards to match
the old ones—a deep reddish stain
our daughter first thought was blood
until we told her it was not blood.

And not our desperation, it was hers.
It was scraped, sanded, varnished.
No one can tell. It could have happened
to anyone, but it happened to us.
We barely knew her. We weren't there.
We didn't want to make their tragedy
our tragedy. It was not our story.
They had their story. We have ours.

Scrabble in Heaven

They're playing Scrabble in heaven
to pass the time, sitting at their usual
places around the table—
or whatever passes for a table there—
my father opposite my mother,
Uncle Al across from Floss,
husband opposite wife—all four of them
bickering as they did in life—
the Scrabble board laid flat
on the wooden lazy Susan,
as Sunday afternoons they'd play
while dinner was cooking,
or if my mother was too tired to cook,
order takeout from the Hong Kong.

After dinner, they'd resume the game,
a conversation interrupted midsentence;
cigarette smoke rising from ashtrays,
dirty dishes stacked in the sink,
chopsticks poking from the trash pail.
They never invited me
to join them. So I'd sprawl on the rug
feeling sorry for myself,
one ear tuned to Ed Sullivan on TV,
one ear tuned to their squabbling,
which continued even when they consulted
the *Webster's* to check a word,

tucking its red ribbon bookmark between
tarnished gilt-edged pages.

Sunday after Sunday,
the lazy Susan rotating on the table,
the pastel squares checkering the grid,
the light blue squares, the navy, the red,
the black star on the pink square
in the dead center of the empty board,
the silky feel of the tiles brushing
fingertips as they select the letters—
just as I'm doing now, touching these keys—
as their memories of the earth
and all the words they had for them—
daughter niece husband wife sister
tree rock dog salt—
diminish one by one.

Gelato

When Caravaggio's Saint Thomas pokes his index finger
past the first knuckle, into the living flesh of the conscious,
perfectly upright Jesus Christ, His bloodless wound
like a mouth that has opened slightly to receive it, the vaginal folds
of parting flesh close over the man's finger as if to suck,

that moment after Christ, flickering compassion,
helps Thomas touch the wound, calmly guiding
the right hand of His apostle with His own immortal left,
into the warm cavity, body that died and returned to the world,
bloodless and clean, inured to the operation at hand
and not in any apparent pain—

to accidentally brush against His arm
would have been enough, but to enter the miraculous flesh,
casually, as if fishing around in one's pocket for a coin—

because it's in our natures to doubt,
I'd doubt what I was seeing, too.

Drawing closer, Thomas widens his eyes
as if to better absorb the injury, his three companions also
strain forward, I do, too,
and so would you, all our gazes straining toward
the exquisite right nipple so beautifully painted I ache to touch
or to kiss it, press my lips to the hairless chest of a god.
His long hippie auburn hair falls in loose
girlish corkscrew curls, the hairs of His sparse mustache

straggle over His upper lip, face so close that Thomas must surely
feel Christ's breath ruffling his brow.

The lecturer closes his notebook and we exit the auditorium.
Conveyed smoothly on the moving sidewalk, as if on water,
but not water,
whooshed through the long, shimmery tunnel connecting
the east and west wings of the National Gallery,
my friend and I hurtle away from the past, that open wound,
and toward the future—

the dark winter colors saturating my eyes suddenly
blossom into the breezy pastels of Italy's gelato,
milk sherbet quick-frozen and swirled
into narrow ribbons of cold rainbow
unbraided into separate chilled stainless steel tubs set
under glass in a cooler case:

                              tiramisù, zabaglione, zuppa inglese,
milky breasts whipped, rippled peach and mango, pistachio,
vanilla flecked with brown dizzying splinters of bean,
coffee, caramel, hazelnut, *stracciatella,*
raspberry, orange, chocolate, chocolate mint; silken peaked
nipple risen from the middle of the just barely opened
undisturbed tub of lemon so pale it's almost white,
scraped with a plastic doll's spoon,
scooped and deposited on the tongue,
then melting its soothing cooling balm.

Acknowledgments

Versions of these poems first appeared in the following publications:

NEW POEMS
Contemporary American Poetry: A Bread Loaf Anthology, ed. Michael Collier and Stanley Plumly: "A Reminder." *Kaimana: The Journal of the Hawaii Literary Arts Council*, 2011: "Danny Kaye at the Palace." *The New Republic*: "Mirror/Mirror." *Ploughshares*: "Fortune Cookies," "Pickwick." *Salmagundi*: "Priorities," "Willow," "Chatty Cathy," "Gaslight," "Staging Your House." *Slate*: "Last Words." *Wooden Teeth*: "American Girls." *The Yale Review*: "Rainbow Weather."

EYE LEVEL (1977)
Audience: "Home Movies: 1949," "The Lifeguard." *The Iowa Review*: "Noon." *The New Republic*: "Fortunes Pantoum," "Witness." *Poetry*: "A Letter Sent to Summer."

This volume was the third recipient of the Juniper Prize, presented annually by the University of Massachusetts Press for a volume of original poetry.

My gratitude to the Radcliffe Institute and to the Massachusetts Endowment for the Arts and Humanities for their support.

THE MINUTE HAND (1987)
The Antioch Review: "A Clock," "A Luna Moth," "Wood." *The Iowa Review*: "High Holy Days." *The New Republic*: "Dresses," "The Glass Slipper," "Persian Miniature," "Pharaoh." *Pequod* (Secret Destinations: Writers on Travel): "The Island." *Ploughshares*: "Anthony," "The Russian Doll." *Poetry*: "Tender Acre," "Young Woman on the Flying Trapeze." *The Seattle Review*: "Thumbelina." *The Yale Review*: "The Game of Jack Straws."

This volume was the 1986 Lamont Poetry Selection of the Academy of American Poets. Judges for 1986: Philip Booth, Louise Glück, and Mary Oliver.

My gratitude to the National Endowment for the Arts and the New York Creative Artists Public Service Program (CAPS) for their support.

MUSIC MINUS ONE (1996)
The G. W. Review: "Missing." *Her Face in the Mirror: Jewish Women on Mothers and Daughters,* ed. Faye Moskowitz (Beacon Press, 1994): "The Bad Mother." *Ploughshares:* "Monday," "Workout." *The Virginia Quarterly Review:* "Music Minus One," "Washing the Streets of Holland."

This volume was a finalist for the 1996 National Book Critics Circle Award.

My gratitude to the John Simon Guggenheim Foundation, the Alfred Hodder Foundation, the National Endowment for the Arts, and George Washington University for their support.

HAPPY FAMILY (1999)
Contemporary American Poetry: A Bread Loaf Anthology, ed. Michael Collier and Stanley Plumly (Middlebury College Press, 1999): "Happiness." *The George Washington Magazine:* "Fairbanks Museum and Planetarium." *A New England Anthology,* ed. Robert Pack and Jay Parini: "Fairbanks Museum and Planetarium." *Pequod:* "Reprise," "The Uncanny." *Salmagundi:* "Mrs. Hitler," "Shit Soup."

A YES-OR-NO ANSWER (2008)
The New Yorker: "Possession." *Pequod:* "Trouble Dolls." *Ploughshares:*
"My Mother's Foot," "Trick Candles." *Princeton University Library
Chronicles,* vol. 63, nos. 1–2 (Autumn 2001–Winter 2002), ed. C. K.
Williams: "The Closet," also published in *Poets of the New Century,*
ed. Roger Weingarten and Richard Higgerson (David R. Godine,
2001). *Salmagundi:* "My Father's Visits," "The Streak." *Tikkun:* "Body
and Soul." *TriQuarterly:* "Gelato." *The Women's Review of Books:* "My
Mother's Chair," "Scrabble in Heaven."

This volume won the Poet's Prize (2010). My gratitude to the twenty-
two judges/poets who chose it, and to the Poetry Center of West
Chester University, which administered the prize.

SPECIAL THANKS
Barry Goldensohn, Lorrie Goldensohn, Jody Bolz, Linda Pastan, Ellen
Voigt, Louise Glück, Julie Agoos, Nadell Fishman, Stanley Plumly, and
to my editor, Michael Collier.

DEDICATIONS
"Where to Find Us" to David Wyatt.
"The Advent Calendar" to Peggy Rizza.
"Eye Level" to Mary Sheldon.
"The Bad Mother" to Rhea Wilson.
"The Sound of Sense" to Ann Moulton.
"The Streak" to Tim Averill.
"My Mother's Foot" to Stanley Plumly.
"Fugue" to Carole E. Horn.
"Gelato" to Michael Fried and Jill Phillips.